TSO AND LA

VIKRAMAJIT RAM was born and educated in Bangalore. After graduating in 1990 from the National Institute of Design, Ahmedabad, he worked for several years as a graphic designer. His first book, *Elephant Kingdom: Sculptures from Indian Architecture* (Mapin, 2007), is a cultural history of the Indian elephant, told through depictions of the animal in ancient art. It was followed by a travelogue, *Dreaming Vishnus: A Journey through Central India* (Penguin, 2008). He is presently at work on another history.

Tso and La

A Journey in Ladakh

VIKRAMAJIT RAM

HarperCollins *Publishers* India

First published in India by
HarperCollins *Publishers* in 2012

Building 10, Tower A, 4th Floor, DLF Cyber City, Phase II,
Gurugram Haryana – 122002, India
www.harpercollins.co.in

2 4 6 8 10 9 7 5 3

Page 233 is an extension of the copyright page

P-ISBN: 978-93-5029-362-1
E-ISBN: 978-93-5029-534-2

Typeset in 11/15 Dante MT at
SURYA

Printed and bound at
MicroPrints India, New Delhi

To
the people
and flora and fauna
of
Ladakh

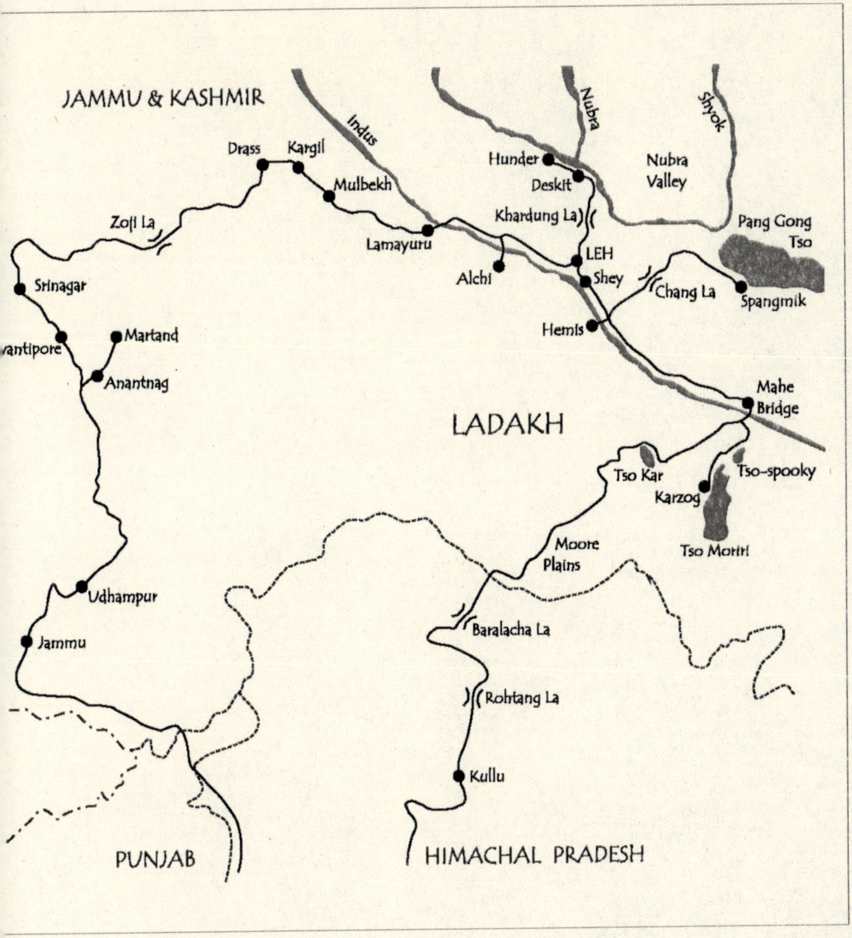

JAMMU & KASHMIR
Indus
Nubra
Shyok
Drass
Kargil
Mulbekh
Hunder
Deskit
Nubra Valley
Khardung La
Zoji La
Lamayuru
Alchi
LEH
Shey
Pang Gong Tso
Chang La
Spangmik
Srinagar
vantipore
Martand
Anantnag
Hemis
Mahe Bridge
LADAKH
Tso Kar
Tso-spooky
Karzog
Moore Plains
Tso Moriri
Udhampur
Baralacha La
Jammu
Rohtang La
Kullu
PUNJAB
HIMACHAL PRADESH

Prologue

The beige leatherette album looks, feels and smells well travelled. The hand rests on the cover for a moment before turning it open. The glassine papers interleafing the black pages lift and settle with a translucent crackle.

Firm in their yellowing corner tabs and captioned in white pencil, the monochromes have mellowed to silver-amber. All date from the short, Himalayan summer of 1957. A frail wooden bridge spans a broad river. Montane treelines advance to cold serrated crags. There are several panoramas of a vast waterbody that may be an ocean. Dark specks in the desolation are people, tents, yaks or outcrops; it's hard to tell.

Groupings of men occupy other frames – tight as a unit and smiling raffishly for the camera. Late twenties and thirties, they are kitted in army-regulation boots and woollens. Their numbers remain reassuringly constant across the pages. Trim-moustached visages come to sport full wild beards; brows have creased and darkened from squinting long and hard into the horizon; goggles and flapping overcoats provide more clues to conditions. One still life, strangely moving, recalls two enamel mugs on a windowsill overlooking a snow-clad vista. There are individual portraits too, inscribed by comrades-in-arms. The captions indulge flashes of whimsy. A 'Highland Beauty' in jewelled headgear and outlandish robes shares page-space with a severe bare-bosomed matron. Elsewhere, a highland chief (from his garb) poses with the album's owner (then a Captain) who is similarly attired. Now in his eighties, the Colonel is in his living room. The house in this leafy New Delhi neighbourhood is cool and quiet; May 2009, outside, is witheringly fierce. The album is balanced on an armrest between us. Together, we've slowly perused the whole collection. I ease back the pages to the waterbody, identified in the caption as 'Pang Gong Tso'.

'Colours,' whispers the Colonel, brushing the views lightly with the back of his hand. The hand lifts like a bird, hovers and alights softly back onto the page. A botched procedure last summer has stolen a vocal cord, so there's a forced economy to his words. He turns with that disarming smile. 'In the water. Tell me about them when you return.'

It will be several days before his son and I arrive at Pang Gong. Tso is Tibetan-Ladakhi for 'lake'. La is the word for 'mountain pass'. We must touch a high La and from there descend to the astounding silence that is the lake. Perhaps it is the salinity of its water, glazed by the chill sun, that causes the colours that fill it to the brim. I spend our first afternoon there assigning names to some.

There's a moonshine blue and an Ella blue. An emerald blue and a jade blue. Ming and Wedgwood, pharaonic and feather, lightning and nightmare, dolphin, mystic, flambé, cold-love. A surprise permanganate of purple turns celadon, in turn saturating as verdigris neon. I drag my eyes back to our pebble beach when a clamour of brown-headed gulls congregates near the Colonel's son (hereafter referred to by a diminutive of his name) who has perched himself upon a rock.

The neptune of Man's jacket matches a plume of that hue in the water. He raises his camera; the gulls lift into the breeze as one, battle the current, and land bolder and closer. My travelling companion has a knack for perfectly framing birds on the wing. Another penchant, for running marathons, extends to motoring: he has driven us up from Bangalore and the drive down remains. The gulls suddenly take to the water. Man turns with a laugh. I issue a mock-regal wave and return to my nomenclature of blues.

The opposite shore seems an eternity away. Where the water meets its hem of ashen ranges is a blade-sharp line of colour so intense it wouldn't care a damn if it were named or not. I stare at it for ages, then lie back against my rock. The sky is transparent alabaster. I shut my eyes against it all.

This journey, summer 2009, has no agendas: no work-in-progress or proposed-work, no arcane quest or fact-finding mission. Each day thus far has been shaped by timing and chance, not by minute planning and research. The old album – it had emerged without ceremony – is a very good example.

Another is Yangchan Dolma's thermos of *kahwa* for Khardung La.

The lone fire horse, thundering past in a smoke of green dust.
Finding the soft-crumbling Sun Temple of Martand.
Dangling in a stuck trolley over the Indus.
The Chamber of Painted Bodhisattvas.
The memorials to fallen soldiers.
The kindness of strangers.
The bleating *mok-moks*.
The chatty road signs.
Garrulous gulls ...
A lot can happen under rarefied conditions.

1

8.04 p.m. In a sort of foyer, a man and a woman are seated close, but not touching, in front of a television, their faces wetly blue from its glow. The evening is clammy and layered in browns. The man has on a singlet and shorts. She is in a skirt and tight fitting blouse. I must shout to be heard above the News: can a room be had?

The hotel is set very slightly away from the main action of NH-8 – away from the hard headlong rush of headlights, the monstrous shadows around the roadside tea shacks, the cold neon signboards over the grim faced motels, the fug of dust and exhaust hanging like bad luck over this unnameable shantytown somewhere between Ghodbunder, Maharashtra and Vadodara, Gujarat.

The twosome before the television looks up with blank eyes. The man turns his attention back to the box; the woman levers herself up with a finger on his shoulder. Her outfit complements the crumpled walls of the foyer.

Room is available. Four hundred for the night. Come.

I follow her down a corridor at the far end of which she pushes open a door and flicks on a tubelight.

The room is sky-blue, rendered more unpleasant by the sterile white fluorescence. A metal double-bed with a bare mattress and two pillows is pushed, horribly, along the length to a wall. There are two of us, I mutter, and wonder what need there was to furnish that.

Seven hundred for two. Both men?

I walk very quickly without looking back or around – out through the corridor and the foyer and into the dark overgrown garden where Man is waiting inside the third member of our three-member cast without whom Man and I couldn't have got this far and without whom we can go no further or, for that matter, anywhere at all. This indispensable character is a near-two-tonne silver-and-black SUV-not-car of Japanese manufacture. His name, P. Singh, is more a nod to the part-Sikh roots of his owner, Man, than to the variant of automobile to which he belongs.

'Let's get out of here.'

'You look like you bumped into Norman Bates's mum.'

'Worse; you don't want to know.'

When we finally find more convivial accommodation further up the NH-8, P.Singh's odometer – 023180 when we set out at 4 a.m. from Bangalore – has touched 024257. It is no small achievement that Man's driven 1,077 kilometres in sixteen hours (including pit stops for breakfast, lunch, teas and pees). We are seated like strangers now across a table, warm Cokes and slow service at hand in the outdoor restaurant of the motel. P.Singh is safe in the parking lot in front – his ample boot loaded to keep us on the road for a good month.

It had all begun with an invitation, extended casually enough six weeks ago in the course of a walk in the countryside with our Sunday group of runners and walkers.

The reason for Man walking, not running, the past few months was an ankle in recovery from damage incurred during a game of basketball with his sons. We'd got talking. He told me he had read something I'd written, and how liberating and energizing and daunting it was for him to have quit work some months earlier to explore his yen for (a) motoring (b) photography and (c) birding. He planned to drive, solo, to Ladakh as soon as the passes opened in summer. He had never been there before; would I like to go along if he did?

'Certainly,' I had replied without a moment's hesitation. Anything to distance myself from a novel-in-progress which I hated myself for having ever begun. Anything for respite from dull unimaginative eternal work-in-progress Bangalore. Anything for a proper break from it all with someone else, for a change, doing all the hard work.

'How well do you know this chap?' a male Cassandra in my life wished to know.

'He runs marathons but his ankle is damaged.'

'Left or right?'

I don't see what that has to do with anything. 'Right.'

'Good. He won't be able to drive very fast.'

So here we are, in a shady shantytown somewhere in Maharashtra. All travel, I report to my notebook and warm Coke, is about finding new routes back to the place called home.

For my forty-third last week, my mum gifted me a dual-shell North Face Summit-series jacket.

Yogi got me a Quechua high-altitude, -5° proof, XL, sleeping bag.

Aunt N has seen us off with good-energy vibes.

Taking pity on his gainfully unemployed son, my dad has sponsored a part of my jaunt.

Ryan, who goes filming in high-risk places, has loaned us an enormous red icebox. Minus ice, of course, Redbox will serve as our larder in P.Singh's boot. Supplies therein include granola bars and Knorr soup, a jar each of Marmite and Seville marmalade, Assam tea bags, Nescafé, chocolate and sugar cubes and, underneath this all, a surprise plum cake from Nilgiris, Brigade Road, for Man's forty-seventh; there's no telling yet where we might celebrate the occasion, early June.

It is a very good thing that I like to make lists. A list provides a sense of control over that which one has very little control over. Man had balked at the list I'd drawn up. Nevertheless, a sturdy carton in the boot contains the first-aid box, two thermoses and camp-mugs, enough t.p. to line the Great Wall, ziplock bags and bin liners, candles and matches, a fire extinguisher, a roll of red box tape (never know when it may come in handy) and yards of tough nylon twine. Our Swiss Army knives are on our person. Spectacle cases and sunglasses ride in the glove compartment with P.Singh's papers and an old-faithful compass. A second carton (exclusively Man's department) contains spare bulbs, fanbelts and fuses, cans of brake- and clutch-and-gear fluids, radiator coolant and diesel enhancer, and a spiffy toolbox that has never been used. Our backpacks contain plenty of sunblock but no razors. We've tossed our trekking boots in last with a camera tripod.

The back seat is taken over by maps, birding books, binoculars and cameras. The floor behind us is occupied by two cartons of water bottles, a big bag of apples, and a tray for music, Maglites, spare batteries and mobile phone chargers. I call home to say we are having a very pleasant time. The next call, tomorrow, will be from Jaipur, Rajasthan.

2

In the weeks leading up to this, Man and I had embarked on a get-fitter routine expressly to pre-empt chances of being struck by AMS. No one gets cavalier about Acute Mountain Sickness. Irrespective of whether one flew in or drove up, gradually acclimatizing to gains in altitude, beyond 8,000 feet, AMS doesn't care to be selective.

If nothing else, our daily fix of cardio training has me, for one, feeling lighter in all ways than I have in ages; the face in the mirror has a wicked glow. In order not to appear *too* suave, we've embarked also on Project Beard – Day 3 of which finds us promisingly scratchy and rough. P.Singh too has gone from city-slick to grunge courtesy a patina of dusts (plural) garnered along the Golden Quadrilateral Highway from south India to north India via the western Indian stretch. After two whole days of smooth cruising (barring the approach into Jaipur last evening), we're crawling now through New Delhi's signature traffic snarls. It is 11.20 a.m. Tempers outside are fraying at

42°C; our windows are up and Coldplay is on 'High Speed'. We are staying tonight at Man's parents'. He calls to let them know we'll be there soon; we reach Safdarjung Enclave at 12.40 p.m.

'Your father has already had lunch and is taking a nap,' says Man's mum. 'He's probably heard you and will be getting impatient.'

The first thing to catch my eye in the living room is a rosewood rocking chair of distinctive design, 1940s Modern, a doppelgänger of which resides in my living room. There is also a Keralan male giant with a hot handshake and dazzling smile whose exact role here is not immediately clear.

'Dad's not been too well,' says Man, 'Come along.'

I follow, pausing at a display of military memorabilia. 'These your father's by any chance?'

'Yep.'

I laugh. 'You didn't tell me you were an army brat.'

'I didn't? Anyway. Good afternoon. Here we are.'

The gentleman in the adjustable bed is awake and beams a smile that literally fills the room with light. He reaches up to take his son's hand. They remain like that for a long moment, and then it's time for introductions.

The Colonel's hands are cool and dry. Although barely audible, his words are perfectly formed in what must have been a clipped resonant bass.

'I trust you have had a safe journey so far.'

I make a little joke of the affirmative.

He smiles again. 'I should think so; after all, who taught him to drive.'

His grip tightens as he tries to lever himself up. The Keralan nurse is at once by his side.

A different room seems not to have undergone very many changes since its original occupant set out from home. The bookshelf in the wall is tight with Kiplings and Corbetts, L'Amour, Fleming, Hesse, Smith and Wodehouse. The Rowlings, vividly self-conscious, are no doubt contributions of the grandsons when they stop by from and to their boarding school in the hills. On the opposite wall, a pink nude-on-canvas is terrified by her reflection in a fish pool.

'Did he paint the masterpiece?' I ask Man's mum.

'Good lord, no,' she laughs, extracting a weathered bomber jacket from a wardrobe. 'I mustn't forget; he wants to take this with him tomorrow.'

There is a framed photograph of the family, younger, together. Chip off the old block. Before I can stop myself, the words tumble out: 'How long has it been?'

'You mean ... Ah. Six months. The doctors say he is making good progress. Terribly strong willed, you see. He's told himself he'll make a complete recovery. So each day, he feels a little bit better.'

She drapes the jacket on a chair, brushing a thread off the

fleece collar. 'See that sleeping bag? It was issued when he went to Ladakh. Before we got married.'

In September 1957, an Indian Army patrol on routine surveillance at Pang Gong Tso stumbled upon unexpected goings-on in a section of the neighbouring Aksai Chin plateau – an inhospitable high-altitude wasteland, administered by India (south of the Johnson-Ardagh Line) and by the People's Republic of China (north of the Mcartney-MacDonald Line). That a road was under construction on the Chinese side was patently clear. It might not have mattered too much, except that it ran uncomfortably close to the Indian side of the Pang Gong region.

The report submitted to New Delhi by the Indian patrol – to which Man's father belonged – was confirmed almost a year later, in July 1958. By then, the People's Liberation Army of China had completed a highway which it had, in fact, begun work on in March 1956. Evidence, this time, came in the form of printed Chinese maps which not only showed the 750 mile-long road linking the Xinjiang-Uyghur Autonomous Region of China to the Tibet Autonomous Region of China, but also claimed the whole of Aksai Chin as Chinese territory.

India was prompt to confront Peking via diplomatic channels on this discrepancy, and when nothing came of dialogue, dispatched two different patrols to Pang Gong to reconnoitre the highway. Both patrols were detained by the Chinese and released after a month. Continued skirmishes, thereafter, escalated into the Sino-Indian war of 1962. On the twentieth of

October that year, Pang Gong witnessed action between the Indian Army and the People's Liberation Army of China.

'Did you go there again in '62?' We are gathered for tea in the living room.

The Colonel flashes an annoyed look. 'No. I would have liked to.'

I must sound woefully naïve. 'What was it like in '57?'

The words are lost. I lean a little closer. 'I was twenty-seven.'

What was I doing at twenty-seven? Eminently forgettable. 'How did all of you travel up?'

'Trucks. Jeeps. Mules. And on foot.' A pause. 'Old bridle trails.'

'Did anyone carry a camera?'

A soundless chuckle. 'We *all* carried cameras.' He makes a little gesture. 'Rolleiflex. Black and white. Agfa. Did not spoil. The cold. Months to wait. To develop and print.'

'And ... the lake?'

'And the lake.' His eyes twinkle. 'There is an album.'

3

It has been established fairly early that much of this drive will be taken in silence. That Man has chosen to captain P.Singh for the entire length of the journey has been most prudent: he knows his wheels best. This seat, therefore, is perfect for navigation, introspection and reflection without my jeopardizing anyone or anything.

Since exiting Delhi at 4 a.m. we have made excellent progress, through Karnal, Kurukshetra, Ambala, Ludhiana and Jalandhar, to sail now along NH-1A. It is a little past ten. A scenic stretch of the Punjab countryside is made up, almost exclusively, of acres upon acres of sunflower and wheat fields, interspersed with little market towns overflowing with fruit markets. Aside from trucks manned by fierce bearded truckers, the odd inter-state bus and mini-van, the highway is very much ours. An avenue of eucalyptus trees has hundreds of numbered and colour-coded bee-boxes in the shade; the mid-morning air is honey-balmed. At a dhaba outside Hoshiarpur – my first authentic Punjabi dhaba – we make an early lunch of the world's best aloo parathas, served up with dollops of butter and washed down with cool foot-long lassis. Back on the highway, a road sign reads *Do not be rash end in crash*. It prompts a reflection on Man's driving.

His confidence is borne not by bravado or any desire to chalk up distances, but rather, keen reflexes and impeccable road sense. We've covered some 1,000 miles to date of largely unfamiliar terrain, almost all of it at a stately forty to fifty mph, and not once has P.Singh's klaxon been employed; it is unlikely that it ever will. We never tailgate. Nor are we prone to nudging or bullying. Behemoths who extend us the right of way are acknowledged with a wave of Man's hand. His impatience with less discerning road-users is expressed by a curl of the lip and a string of expletives – muttered, of course.

To offset such quirks, Man drives for the most part with a mildly delinquent smile. If his tastes in cabin music are eclectic, he cannot hold a tune to save his life. He can go for hours without sustenance, so long as water and Polo mints are near at hand. At the close of each drive, he must meticulously log our mileage, driving-time and average speed; in the weeks to come, temperature and altitude will also be thrown in. Having thus conveyed us safely from one place to the next, he enters an inviolate zone for about forty-five minutes during which I am left to my own devices. This mainly involves scribblings in my notebook of the day's happenings, with a separate section for totting up bills that will someday be shared.

At a little roadside shrine, next, a priest offers us some sweetened puffed-rice and a dab of vermillion to our foreheads.

The dab is cooling; the temperature outside is 37°C. By late afternoon, the landscape and the air over it have altered. A climb is announced by a signboard urging drivers to *Be mild on my curves 7,873 feet*. The mountainside begins as a mix of oleander, silk cotton, shisham and mango trees, turning to copses of pine along the highest reach. The descent down the other side swings past a lake bobbing with paddleboats, scattered groups of people on the grassy banks. An inordinately long bridge transports us across the river Ravi. Without quite realizing it, we seem to have entered Jammu & Kashmir. The premise is soon confirmed at a border checkpost.

At the drop-gates, some men are working their way along the lines of vehicles on either side, checking documents and the contents of cabins and boots. Waiting for our turn, I turn on my mobile phone to keep Bangalore up to speed on our current co-ordinates.

The device, fully charged and serviceable yesterday, appears to have inexplicably expired; no amount of switching off and on again can persuade it to connect.

'Try mine,' says Man.

'Dead too.' It's as though some invisible force has conspired to cut off all communication links with the world outside of Jammu and Kashmir; I'm not exactly complaining. When it's our turn at the barricade, the policeman running the check informs us, in a matter of fact manner, that mobile connections registered outside Jammu & Kashmir cease to function within the boundaries of the state, expressly in the interest of state and national security. In one fell swoop, our phones have been turned into devices for telling the time.

It is 6.11 p.m. when we reach Udhampur. Man, in characteristic style, springs another surprise of the military kind. He'd had a word, sometime yesterday, with a cousin in the army. Courtesy the good offices of said kinsman, our digs for tonight are in a high-security transit camp in Udhampur Cantonment. By seven, we've been cleared by an elaborate series of checks and barricades and waved on to an A-Category Guesthouse attached to the Officers' Mess. A-Class comforts, thereafter, have extended to a five-course dinner laid out by a uniformed orderly in an A-Class family suite.

Despite a perfectly restful night, I'm in a blue funk this morning – the sort that has me convinced that if something is to go wrong, it will do so today. In the effortless way of these things, my unspoken sense of unease has transferred itself to my friend; the silence inside P.Singh feels different. The only explanation for the anxiety I can think of is that it's imperative we reach Srinagar before tonight.

Around half-ten and roughly eighty kilometres into the drive, we have our first glimpse, from the little town of Chandrakote, of a range of distant snowpeaks. The oppressive mood inside P.Singh shifts a little, but not enough. At noon, beyond Nowgam, a signboard across NH-1A announces the start of the three-kilometre-long Jawahar Tunnel through the mountain ahead.

Within seconds of entering it, we are engulfed in pitch blackness – but only for a moment, before the reflectors lining the sides of this engineering feat become a string-course of flickering red, drawing us closer and closer to an ever widening dot of light. The sun when we emerge is blinding. Sweeping away to the side of the highway and backed by an eternity of distant snowpeaks lies the summer-kissed Vale of Kashmir.

4

Lied about not researching our destination, specifically for crumbling treasures of the architectural kind. The last thing the evening before the morning of departure, I dashed out with my Penguin/Michell to run up photocopies of the first section: northern India. From the map therein, I have memorized the general location of one particular antique site.

'There is a place called Martand nearby,' I tell Man over my paratha. Not quite as good as the ones yesterday but still. We have stopped for lunch at a place called Wanpoo on the highway to Srinagar. It's just the dhaba owner and us and a pond giddy with lotuses.

'What about it?'

'There's a temple there that we should check out.'

'Ah; not too keen on those.'

'This one's different.'

'In what way?'

Keep the excitement out of your voice. 'I don't know. We'll find out.'

He contemplates this over his lassi.

'It's ancient,' I add. Just uttering the word brings on that old frisson; it's been a while since I've indulged this sort of thing. Déjà vu. The feeling passes, in the perplexing way of all déjà vu. I'm warming to my theme. 'Not quite as colossal as Konark. Between that and the one in Modhera, but still huge.'

'I'm lost.'

'A temple to the sun god. Like the other two, completely in ruins. And older; eighth century.'

'And you think it's somewhere here.'

'I *know* it is. The sun temple of Martand.'

Man: *'Achha bhaiyya, suno. Yahan aas-paas mey koi purana mandir hai? Martand?'*

Dhaba man: *'Mattan? Ji haan, sir ji. Is road pe thhoda aagey Khanabal junction milega. Wahan se Anantnag ki taraf right turn lijiye. Mattan milega Anantnag se aath-das kilometre aagey.'*

A stroke of luck we haven't overshot. 'You see?'

'He said Anantnag. That would be *the* Anantnag.'

'I know; bummer.' Second largest city after Jammu and occasional target (like other parts of this embarrassingly lyrically paradisiacal valley) of insurgency, clashes, bomb blasts, landmines, shoot-outs and encounters. And, somewhere near it, a crumbling monument to an indestructible force of life.

Man is studying something in his lassi. It is perfectly understandable; I can't expect everyone to share my thing for tumbledown antiquities. Still, knowing we are so near ...

'Pakka?' I ask the dhaba owner, *'Martand surya mandir?'*

'Bilkul, sir ji. Mattan surya mandir.'

A flock of sheep skips by. It's Martand, I inwardly correct Mr Lotus Dhaba; all you chaps can think of is bloody mutton.

'You really want to go there, don't you?'

'We don't have to do anything.' I wave it aside with a little shrug.

'Right. Let's go.'

The garden gnome in the *firan* is waiting to cross the road with a thicket of willows for his backdrop. We have pulled up for directions. Having pumped my hand through the window, he continues to clutch it in his paws – a term used advisedly, considering their fur quotient.

The gnome smells overpoweringly of undercooked lamb. I want my hand back, but he continues to shake and squeeze it warmly. '*Mattan? Aagey se right, phir Anantnag se aur aagey. Hum bhi aoo?*'

Thank you, I tell him, quickly divesting my hand. And sorry, we have no room for hitchhikers.

It's the same pronouncement from a different firan-clad gent at the turn-off to Anantnag: '*Mattan? Seedha, takreeban bees kilometre.*'

And again on high street, Anantnag – all half-timbered architecture and people and vehicles – where a unit of men in uniform has clambered with supplies into the back of its truck. 'Correct road. Proceed straight. Turn right near the chashme shahi.'

I thank the men and return to P.Singh. 'What on earth is a chashme shahi?'

'A spring. Why?'

'They said it's near one of those. *Quelle* picturesque.'

Which, despite a backdrop of powder-blue mountains, cannot be said for the road out of Anantnag: a depressing drag of business and residential districts, serially arranged, with names that ring vaguely familiar from reports in print and on television each time there's an 'incident'. Gradually, the shanties start to fall back. The air breathes a sigh of relief. A large signboard tacked to a chainlink fence announces the chashme shahi to our left.

It is a stretch of pebble beach with swift-flowing whitewater behind a curtain of willow trees. All very pretty indeed. But I am perturbed by a different sign:

MATTAN – 0 KM

In these parts, I tell myself, they probably spell the way they speak. Or perhaps the sign-painter had no English and happily decided to go phonetic. Or maybe it's a typo; mistakes occur all the time, how dull to be always perfect. Somehow I'm not too convinced. This does not auger well. Not one bit.

'Something wrong?' says Man, mind-reader. We are rolling along in second gear.

'Nothing.'

'This is the place, right?'

'Oh yes. Only the name is a bit … different.'

He gives me a quick look. 'Meaning what, exactly?'

'The place we need is m-a-r-t-a-n-d.'

He brakes. 'But … all those chaps … you checked …'

'Precisely. Tell you what. If we don't find the temple in the next few minutes, we'll turn right round and pretend none of this ever happened.'

Man mutters something that sounds like fuckpriceless and

noses P.Singh into a diagonally backwards-facing road to the right. A signboard in the corner there reads MATTAN SURYA MANDIR. There is indeed a temple a short way ahead. There is also a sinking feeling in my tum.

The pink-washed walls of the temple-complex are plastered with posters of politicians and latter-day Hindu saints. An arch welcomes all comers to the Mattan Sun Temple; several red-orange buildings are ranged behind the closed double-gates. Some officious types are controlling a squash of lesser mortals streaming in as well as emerging through a picket gate to the side. The ones that are going in bear trays full of offerings. The shops along the road are doing brisk business.

Man's face is set in a particular expression, not quite a scowl but close, that has caused his eyebrows to dart up as vexed peaks. He manoeuvres us into a vacant slot between two parked taxis. Some louche hangabouts pass a comment which I hope, for their sake, he hasn't heard.

'I'll wait,' he snaps, 'Go ahead.'

There's nothing for it. I collect my camera and head for the gate. Even before stepping through, I know this sun temple is not my sun temple.

Ahead of the reception zone, an expanse of flat ground is worked into a grid of square pools and paved walkways. Many of the visitors, coursing this way and that, have stopped to feed the trout flashing in the dark depths. At the far end is a tree-filled ridge with a row of white shrines. Not one of them is a crumbling monument. I find myself jostled forward towards a kiosk where footwear must be deposited.

'I am looking for the sun temple of Martand,' I say to the man there.

'It is that one,' he replies, 'The one in the middle.'

'No; the one I'm looking for is very *badey, tootey-phootey, bahut puraney*. And ASI.'

The acronym works like a talisman. It always does. Good olde Archaeological Survey.

'Oh *that*,' the man says, 'That one is on the hill behind. Go out and follow the road thataway.'

Breaking the latest to my pal outside is going to be a bloody awful pain. Or just plain bloody. I turn and squint back across the pools. Damn.

Man is at the head of the walkways – gesticulating furiously for me to come back.

We are making gentle loops up a wooded hillside, rendered more beautiful than it already is by maple-like chinars in new leaf. Our windows are down. The air is brushed with a hint of resin. Yet, as unobtrusive reminders of the reality of this setting, in dappled shadows at regular intervals is an armed man in camouflage and hard-helmet. Each one of them glances, almost instinctively, first at our number-plate as we pass by. There is even a bunker of sandbags where the road meets the top of the forested hill.

The crest is an emerald tableland with a terraced rose-garden cascading to one side. Watching over it is the Sun Temple of Martand, softly crumbling in the afternoon light.

Lalitaditya Muktapida's celebratory monument to the sun god radiates distinct Hellenistic leanings. Not surprising. This powerful king of the Karkota dynasty was known well beyond the boundaries of eighth-century India. Among the gifts conveyed by itinerant chroniclers, and emissaries from Central Asia and the Mediterranean may have been references, visual as well as literary, to the imperial splendours of Rome and Greece. The Forum Romanum, certainly, and the Parthenon; the temples of Zeus at Olympia, Poseidon at Sounion and other marvels of their ilk. A myriad other explanations must exist for elements from such originals to have found reinterpretation, in limestone, in a temple to Surya in the heart of Kashmir. Yet the idea of a visiting cultural attaché to Lalitaditya's capital, Parihasapur, planting an architectural seed that would one day bloom into this astonishing edifice, holds particular appeal as I stand in its quiet, grass-carpeted peristyle.

The vast, rectangular courtyard is enclosed by a high plinth. Ranged upon it along one side is a row of fluted columns, varying from eight to thirteen feet in height, in imitation Greek-Doric. Behind the colonnade, a narrow gallery courses past several empty cells that may have originally served as subsidiary shrines. The low, tri-lobed arches into each cell are in turn framed by angled, Classical pediments.

Of the eighty-four columns that originally sprung from the plinth, a little over a dozen still stand, with traces of entablature (in the correct, Classical order of architrave, frieze and cornice) still discernible between the columns that have survived. Everything is ravaged by time; the damage could just as easily be the work of a giant rat. In the grass at the base of the plinth lies a profusion of carved masonry fragments, all tumbled from the galleries as well as the main feature in the peristyle.

The temple-proper – massive and utterly in ruins – looms from a rectangular plinth, accessed, from the west, by a broad flight of steps. The overall composition is altogether eccentric – a strange amalgam of Classical and Hindu elements and themes. The most striking features are three towering, tri-lobed archways, serially arranged to distinguish the zones within: the first archway, into the antechamber; the second, into the sanctuary; the third, defining the rear, eastern face of the sanctuary and the temple itself.

Two more archways of similar scale and profile open from the north and south of the sanctuary. All five arches are flanked by Classical pilasters, capped by pyramidal pediments which have almost completely collapsed. Arranged one above the other alongside the pilasters are small, double-gabled frames containing bas relief carvings of many-armed gods and goddesses. More divinities occupy pedimented frames along the basement plinth. The crowned figures, some of them seated on thrones, are compactly built and have squishy features. That they bear lotuses, conches, maces and machetes places them squarely in the Vaishnava pantheon, but because they are so worn, it is hard to accurately distinguish each incarnation or deity.

The roof of the temple – believed to have been of timber and steeply double-gabled – no longer exists, so the antechamber and the sanctuary are open to the sky. The walls and doorjambs carry large bas relief panels in pyramidal frames. Although a lot worse for wear and veiled with cobwebs, the figures here are more readily recognizable than the ones outside, fully exposed to the elements.

The river-goddess Ganga is posed sensuously on her vehicle, a crocodile, clutching a slender lotus stalk in her principal right hand and a water-pot in her principal left. One of two female attendants holds an umbrella high over the goddess's head; the other bears a yak-tail flywhisk. The river-goddess, Yamuna, in the neighbouring panel, is similarly modelled on her vehicle, a tortoise.

The panels in the north wall, facing the river goddesses, carry two representations of Vishnu. Each image is three-faced: the central one presumably depicting the god in his principal form, flanked by the faces of Varaha the Boar and Narasimha the Man-Lion. Both figures are eight-armed; their principal right hands rest on the heads of crouching chauri bearers. There are suggestions of more figural carvings and ornament in the lintel of the doorway into the sanctuary. But because of the light spilling in from above, the lintel itself is in silhouette.

The sanctuary is empty. There's no telling what form the icon installed here had taken. I am tempted to believe it was not at all an image in the usual sense but something profoundly metaphoric and grandly dramatic. A mirror, or mirrors, of some sort, perhaps, on a central axis, perhaps, to catch the rays of the sun and –

My whimsical vision abruptly ends there. I turn and look out through one of the archways.

Man is walking in the colonnaded gallery outside. He stops now and then, composing frames in his camera with great concentration. So much for not being too keen on temples. I smile wryly to myself and turn and wander back towards the first archway.

The view from the top of the stairway presents the forecourt of the temple, with a square ceremonial stepped-tank in the grass between these steps and the main gateway into the complex. The tank, not very deep, is empty. The gateway – all pilasters and carved jambs – is almost as monumental as the temple and just as derelict. Great ceremonial processions must have once coursed through it. Lalitaditya would have ridden in on an elephant. I sit on the topmost step and open my photocopies from Penguin/Michell.

On either side of the doorway behind me had once stood two large shrines. Only parts of their masonry walls remain, set away from the main temple by a few feet and tipping slightly to the sides; one giant shrug and they'll topple in a heap. A random thought, something to do with an earthquake, is itching to reveal itself. It is prevented from doing so by a voice behind me: 'Would you like a guided tour?'

The man, dapper and middle-aged, has a moustache like a caterpillar at rest between aquiline nose and thin upper lip. He must have been lurking in the shadows all the while I was inside.

'Not particularly,' I reply, pleasantly.

'It is okay,' he sighs. 'Not many outsiders make it here these days.'

We stare at each other in silence for a moment.

'May I take a look at what you are reading?'

'Certainly,' I reply, handing him the photocopies.

He studies them carefully. 'Private or government?'

'Private. Tourist.'

'It is hard for me,' he continues, 'to come by material such as this. This scale-plan, as you can see, is accurate. And all these other sites: Masrur, Avantipur, Bunniyar, Harwan, Parsapora, Payar, Ushkur … all quite close by. Do you plan to visit all of them? I can take you, if you are interested.'

'Just Martand for now; I'll save the rest for the next time.'

'In that case, would you mind very much if I keep these? They will come in useful in my line of work.'

'All yours,' I say. 'And what do you do?'

'Nothing,' he says, with a diffident smile. 'There is nothing to do these days.'

With that, he starts down the stairway, poring through the pages. Not a very smart thing letting them go; it will mean having to muddle through Ladakhi monasteries minus Notes over the following weeks. But too late. I watch the retreating figure and when he is out of sight, try in vain to retrieve an earlier train of thought involving an antique earthquake.

Shortly, Man reappears, very pleased, with a cache of compositions of Graeco-Romanesque details. It is lovely out here: the warm sun, the butterflies inspecting the daisies, the silence. Back at P.Singh – down past the terraced rose-garden with its borders of poppies – I reach up and make a souvenir of a chinar leaf.

5

The Dal Lake is a sheet of slate upon which the morning has drawn a veil of mist. A lone shikara glides by, inscribing a quatrain of ripples. A few joggers are pounding the paved embankment. The shapes in the distance are the dome and minaret of the Hazratbal shrine. The road hugs the edge of the lake, curves past the last of the Raj-era houseboats and the smart district where ministers live before looping upwards and outwards to the Srinagar–Leh Highway.

At this early hour, NH-1D is busy mainly with sheep and goats, their shepherds carrying new lambs in their arms and in shoulder bags. But for the soldiers that are already at position under the trees, it is easy to be lulled into a false sense of security in this idyllic countryside. We arrive in the glen of Sonmarg at eleven.

The approach from here to the pass known as Zoji La is guarded by a police checkpoint. A queue of vehicles has assembled at the barricade. This will lift only after a military convoy has made it over from Drass on the other side; the convoy is expected at 1.30 p.m. The grassy slopes flanking the road are crawling with people who've tumbled out of cars, buses and mini-vans to wait it out under the sharp blue sky. To one side of the road is a line of shops crammed with Kashmiri crewel work and papier mâché souvenirs and Chinese-made high-altitude wear and trekking-gear. I potter around for a bit and then walk over to the police checkpoint.

The men on duty aren't the least bit concerned by the presence, with notebook, of a stranger on their front steps. One of them goes so far as to produce a chair so that I may continue to scribble in comfort at the entrance of the building. Indoors, an interrogation of some sort is underway. Forceful questions; muffled responses. The Urdu of the dialogue is all Greek to my ears so I return, in the notebook, to Srinagar last evening.

We hadn't stopped, after Martand, at the ruins of Avantipore right beside NH-1A, instead keeping an even pace down an achingly beautiful wooded stretch of the highway, our passage noted, along the way, by soldiers in camouflage, waiting, just waiting, to pre-empt some ghastliness from erupting. It was with relief, therefore, that we had turned, in Srinagar Cantonment, into another high-security transit camp at which Man's cousin, again, had ensured we'd be provided a room for the night.

The main administrative block was early twentieth century at heart, its gabled façade cloaked in wisteria and fronted by an abundance of full-blown pink roses. The anachronistic air of the exterior had continued inside – the wooden staircase over

Reception creaking and protesting under the back-slapping bonhomie of a troop of hobnailed boots and sharp uniforms, tramping out into the rose-drunk evening. In the sudden hush left in their wake, the quartermaster entering our credentials into a ledger had mumbled something about a dress code in force everywhere on the premises. Civvies were fine, so long as they were presentable and pressed. He had then leant over the front desk and wagged a finger at two pairs of bare legs. It had loosely translated to scurry to your room, scruffies, and stay put there until you must leave. We did just that, pausing at P.Singh for granola bars, water and backpacks.

The room, thereafter, was one of several in a veranda overlooking a further profusion of fragrant pink. A spartan 12'x12' square, it was furnished with two beds with quilts like mattresses in their own right, a table and two chairs. I must have fallen asleep almost immediately, opening an eye at some point to find Man pacing like a stir-crazed zoo exhibit in the narrow strip of carpet between the main door and the bathroom, stopping only when a call to the last prayers of the day had floated over at eight from a mosque somewhere. We had dined then on granola and water, hit the lights and crept under those monumental quilts. At six this morning, an orderly had rapped on our door to say the dress code had been partially relaxed; we were welcome to a buffet breakfast in the Mess before the others descended at seven. That meal, albeit hearty, feels like a very distant memory.

'What are you writing about?' says a friendly voice.

The Kashmiri policeman is built like a lumberjack with spaniel-eyes and a light sandy beard. Unlike the other cops milling in and out of the building, this one carries his beret at a jaunty tilt. The tag pinned to a breast pocket reads *Mq. Ahmed, P.C.*

'This and that,' I reply. 'While we wait to get moving.'

'Travelling alone?'

'No. My buddy is around somewhere.'

'How are you travelling?'

'We've driven up. That's his vehicle over there.'

'We see a lot of your type. Where from?'

'Delhi. No; Bangalore.'

'Make up your mind,' the constable laughs, the corners of his eyes crinkling.

'Bangalore. We plan to exit from the Leh–Manali highway.'

'Any other passengers?'

'No. It's just the two of us.'

The interrogation indoors, meanwhile, has risen in decibel level.

'What's going on inside?' I ask.

'Routine stuff. The buses overload, make a quick buck squeezing in more people than they must. This one's a repeat offender; he'll be at it again sooner or later. *Bas*, this afternoon, I am off home after six weeks to the missus and kids. Five days of rest and then back to this grind. Can I hitch a ride to Drass?'

'Certainly,' I reply.

'Thank you,' he says. 'Care for some tea?'

Before I can say yes, he calls to someone inside. Two glasses of tea appear almost immediately. We sip in silence.

'The barricade will lift in half an hour,' says Ahmed P.C, collecting my empty glass. 'There's a waiting yard on the other side; our boys will look out for you there; I'll find you before the convoy arrives. We'll try and make it up the pass ahead of the rest.'

Very resourceful. A plan that has no doubt been practised.

'Perfect,' I say and set off to find my buddy.

He's sipping tea on the lawns of a restaurant of the tourism board of Jammu & Kashmir.

'We're giving a cop a ride to Drass,' I say. 'Sandwiches?'

'We are?'

'Yep. So. Cheese for you too? Safer than chicken, I should think.'

'Yep.'

'You sure?'

'Yes.'

'He has a wife and children he hasn't seen in ages.'

'Give it a rest,' says Man. Our sandwiches arrive. We wolf them down. At the billing counter, a poster indicates the presence, in Kargil, of a guesthouse of the tourism board.

No reservations required, says the man at the counter, handing back some change. Just land up and ask for a room.

The barricade has been removed at 12.45 p.m., permitting the queue to pass through and into a large open space where everyone is organized in rows, nose to tail. With some help from our constable's comrades, P.Singh is positioned fourth in the lead. Ahmed finds us as he'd promised, and then goes back to the road to join his mates. The military convoy is announced, on the dot of 1.30, by a pilot jeep bearing a red flag. It is followed, in a minute, by a file of forty covered trucks, evenly spaced, with a green-flag jeep bringing up the rear. All around, doors bang shut and engines rev as the first civilian convoy of the day readies itself for the ascent.

'*Chalo*,' says Ahmed, jumping into the back and at once expressing surprise at the paraphernalia with which he's sharing space.

'There's more in the boot,' says Man. 'Help yourself to something to eat.'

'May I have one of these?' asks Ahmed, finding himself a granola bar.

Keep the box. For your children. Biscuits too, if you like.

'Bleeding heart,' mutters Man.

'And what a gorgeous road,' I say.

NH-1D up Zoji La has snaked cleanly up the bare mountainside. Progress up it is slow, nonetheless, single file, rendered slower by the dinky hatchback in front and the buses ahead. No one pips, no one overtakes, there is no traffic from the opposite side. Less than fifteen minutes into the drive, P.Singh has his first, up-close brush with snow and ice; the temperature gauge on the dashboard reads 4°C. Our windows slide up, the heater is turned on. The high way alternates between stretches of impeccable tarmac and stretches of interlocked cobbles of concrete – all courtesy a wing of the army known as the Border Roads Organisation (BRO), the skills of which we will be seeing more of in the weeks ahead.

The ground beyond Man's side of the road has plunged smoothly down as miles of driven white, to climb, far away, as parallel ranges of snowpeaks scarred with bedrock of purple and black. To my left is an endless wall of white, overhung by long daggers of ice. Here too there is graffiti – hearts impaled, names entwined, a daisy, a smiley face, hours and minutes, month and date – carved in icicle-point yesterday and as yet unmelted in this permanently snowbound place.

At 11,630 feet, the summit of Zoji La is an undulating smoothness of blinding intensity, with the opaque matte hardness of royal icing. It is hard to believe that every inch of this seemingly inviolate landscape, its every dip and rise and trough and crest, has been accounted for in numerical values of latitude and longitude, altitude and depth, plane and incline. Yet how hard it is to capture in words the same attributes of height, scale, distance, expanse.

I turn around to find Ahmed asleep, very long lashes and a dreamtime smile, one of our birding books open on his lap. He wakes up when we arrive in Drass, is met by friends, insists on treating us to breadsticks and tea at a roadside café. We part in the hope we meet again someday.

Traffic, meanwhile, has thinned to a trickle of cars and motorbikes. The vast green valley, contained by harsh ranges, is dotted with the softer profiles of houses and horses and people like toys. A little outside Drass, a signboard anticipates the memorial to the heroes of Kargil.

The Bhimbat War Memorial occupies a large clearing by the side of NH-1D, with the Tololing Range for its backdrop. Two sentries are positioned like painted pewter statuettes on either side of the entrance driveway. But for P.Singh, the parking lot is empty and remains that way for the duration of our visit.

At the far end of the driveway are two small buildings – a War Museum and a kiosk with memorabilia for sale. The memorial-proper, on an elevated terrace, is in a Rajput-revivalist architectural style, expressed in pink-sandstone to the walkways, columns and balustrades. The walkways merge at a high wall. Carved into it are the names and ranks of the Heroes of Operation Vijay: 527 soldiers, casualties of Action, May to July 1999, between India and Pakistan on the same, snow-clad range behind the monument. The conflict – provoked by Pakistani infiltrators into the Indian Line of Control in Kargil Valley – had ended in victory for India. For the duration of the Operation and long after it, Tiger Hill and Tololing had become household names, their jagged white profiles beamed live to millions of televisions throughout the subcontinent, and millions more worldwide.

The inside of the Museum is lined with panels of maps, graphics, photographs and text. There is a small shrine in the middle, dedicated by all faiths. On an escritoire by the door are two visitors' books. One is for officers and the other for civilians.

The guesthouse is tucked away at the top of a dark bylane, branched from the high street of Kargil. While one waits in P.Singh, the other goes up to investigate. The place seems to be deserted. The rooms lining the verandas are padlocked; there is no front desk. A weak lightbulb illuminates a passage onto the rear of the building. In the shadows is a ramshackle outhouse, a room upstairs with a light on inside. I take the staircase to the balcony.

The man in the room leaps back with a start from the pot he is stirring on a gas range. I apologize for scaring him and ask for a room for the night.

'There are no rooms to let,' the man replies.

'But the gentleman at your establishment in Sonmarg had assured me there would be and that no reservation was required. Perhaps you could call him from that phone over there? I do have a number for him.'

The man's expression changes from nonplussed to irritated. 'The phone doesn't work,' he says. 'You can have a room, but you'll have to clear out if someone *with* a reservation shows up.'

'In which case,' I say, 'you can unlock any of the other empty rooms for those with reservations.'

Mutter mutter grumble mumble. 'And mind you, there's no food to be had here.'

'What do you suggest as an alternative?'

'You might find something on high street.'

It doesn't sound too promising from what we've seen of the gloomy drag. I don't debate the point in case the bundle of joy changes his mind and decides he won't let us stay. After he's shut off the gas and set the pot aside, I follow him downstairs, give the room on offer a nod of acceptance, and go down to give Man the good tidings. We throw in our things, secure the padlock and set out with a Maglite to the high street.

It is more depressing up-close than the glimpse earlier had suggested: a string of hardware shops and mechanics' and vulcanizers' outfits, all with shutters downed for the day. The few people about glance furtively and quicken their steps; it's as if the soul has been sucked out of this place by the fears and memories it hasn't, ten years on, been able to erase. I'm almost resigned to another feast of granola and water when Man catches sight of a restaurant sign.

We are the only clients in a green upstairs room with a flickering tubelight. A blank-faced young man produces an exclusively non-vegetarian menu – mutton-this, mutton-that, mutton somesuch-something – in which the only recognisable items are 'mutton noodle soup' and 'mutton mok mok'. The soup is passable, so long as one overlooks the gristle, the grit, the floating globules of fat. The mok moks are deep fried and their filling, stringy. With each bite I take, a little lamb bleats piteously inside my head.

The Sun Temple of Martand

P.Singh and Manoj Bawa

Zoji La

The Bhimbat War Memorial at Drass

A mohawk mountain and a gompa

Dhukhang, Lamayuru gompa

Mani cloisters, Lamayuru gompa

Painted chorten, Alchi gompa

House and garden, Alchi

The Alchi Quartet

The langs at the Gangbas, Leh

6

Few signatures of a faith do it with such breezy panache. The prayer flags are Tibetan-Buddhist – a vivid surprise, an impermanent gateway, strung over the deserted road between two tall stakes. They are new, not weathered, flirting with the sun like blue, white, red, green and yellow crystals. Each is a paean to ether, air, fire, water and land, the benedictions of their fabric energizing the wind. My mood lifts the instant we course underneath. Ladakh of the mind's eye has just turned real.

If I were to assign a colour to it, the colour for today would have to be red.

The pin-pricks on a dun slope evoke a rope of ruby beads, suddenly cut loose to roll unrestrained. They are child-monks – tonsured, flappy-robed, rumbustious as puppies – tumbled from a *gompa* on top of the hill. Our timing coincides: the monklings skitter to a stop beside the tarmac. Their voices are clear and high as wind chimes.

'Julley!' they wave, as we slowly course by.

Julley. It's a delightful greeting: variously good-day, welcome, thank you, godspeed. This is our first encounter of it. Coming from these brick-cheeked otherworldlies, the syllables must pack also a blessing. I turn and keep waving till they are out of sight. The monastery on the hill is a madness of prayer flags.

Having started out from Kargil on just tea and biscuits, hopes of a more substantial breakfast are rewarded at Mulbekh. It is a quiet little settlement, sprouted along the upper lip of a valley. A roadside café has a terrace seated with tables and chairs waiting for something to happen. The staff is in no hurry with our omelettes.

Directly across the road is a sun-dredged monolith, a solitary flag fluttering jauntily from its peak. Fronting the rock, a little red-and-white two-storeyed building has its horizontal rooflines strung with *tarchoks*; the doorway is guarded by a gnarled juniper and an animation of vertical *tarchens*. More prayer flags are stretched from the building and the tree to an open pavilion in which stands an enormous prayer wheel. The cylindrical *mani*, some 8 feet in height and as much in circumference, is painted deep claret and embossed with brass and silver medallions and bands. The pavilion itself is painted with Tibetan dragons, fish, and infinite-knot and floral motifs in pastel blue, yellow, mint and white. In the middle of the roof, a smaller mani, formed from an old oil-tin and brightly painted, trundles like a wind vane amidst the tarchoks there. A troop of children in red school uniforms enters the pavilion and circumambulates the mani, thrice, giving it a vigorous twirl at each. They next make for the building, emerging from it in under a minute and proceeding noisily up the road. Breakfast can wait; curiosity has got the better of me.

It is a gompa. The low doorway is frilled with bunting of a duster-cloth tiredness. I leave my shoes outside. A dim antechamber is tight with a distinctive resinous incense. It opens onto a small inner courtyard, enclosed on three sides by the monastery and at the fourth, ahead, by the monolith. I run my eyes slowly up it. Serendipity has brought me before this guardian of the old trade route between Srinagar and Leh. Carved onto it in bas relief is a four-armed Maitreya, the Future Buddha, stiffly posed and about thirty feet tall.

The Bodhisattva sports an elaborate braided headdress, hoop earrings, jewelled necklaces and armlets and bracelets. Snaking down his bare torso is a double-strand of sacred threads. The edges of a scarf have swooshed to the sides in a stony breeze. A beaded waistband trims a dhoti-like garment, the pleats of which cascade between column-like legs. A garland, partly sculpted in the round, reaches down to the shins. The fingers of the principal right hand are set in a *mudra* of meditation. The other hands each clutch a water-jar, a sprig of irises and a loop of prayer beads.

Maitreya wears an inexhaustible smile. At his great eroded feet are small groupings of worshippers, also in bas relief, their own features despaired by time. A signboard nearby provides an indication of age: the rock-cut composition dates from the eighth century. The happenings this Bodhisattva must have witnessed, the litanies addressed, through those silk-route wool-route trade route times; the gompa around him is more recent. Outside, in its chinoiserie shrine, the claret mani is deeply grumbling.

A series of quick switchbacks have swirled us up some 10,000 feet. Ah, the luxury of stopping like this wherever we please to stretch our legs. Man is already at the edge and turns with an exclamation that is lost for the wind. I slowly walk up to his side. Nothing we have read or seen has prepared us for this.

It is not one mountain but seamless corrugations of bare-naked mountains, madly cycloramic, 360°, thrown cheek by jowl like snoring jurassics. Across the sunburnt hide of the nearest, below us, far away, is the undulating claw-scratch that has conveyed us onto this lizardback. Crawling up it now is a red lorry-insect with a blue plastic carapace. A gauze of cloud films the sun, lending a fugitive green filter to the light; the slopes wrinkle and shrink like an expiring breath. This starkness lends itself eagerly to fantasy. If we remain very still, we'll catch a screech of archaeopteryx – heavily leather-winged, out on a scavenge.

Barely half an hour since breakfast but surrealism has made me peckish again. Redbox to the rescue. We fix some crackers and Marmite and lean back in the shade of P.Singh.

This is our day for prayer flags. At 12,198 feet, a concrete signboard on Namik La marks the second-highest point on the Srinagar–Leh highway. Tethered here at waist-height is a superabundance of tarchoks, beating hard staccato incantations to the emptiness; across the valley, a shelf of iced peaks is stiff as meringues. If it were ever harnessed, this wind could keep the subcontinent electrified for posterity. Perish the thought; it seems perfectly happy to be imprinted with charms and entreaties.

Shortly, we pass a mohawk spur with a clutch of ivory and maroon gompas at its base. The roof of one has a gold-yellow pagoda with curlicued eaves. It must be a day of ceremonial significance: some monks on a terrace are raising new prayer flags. The next lot, an hour later on Fotu La, surround a marker at 13,479 feet, their lines dipping and swelling like a carnival tent.

I know a *chorten* when I see one, thanks, really, to *Tintin in Tibet*; so does my fellow aficionado of Hergé. We remember to keep to the left of it and walk around it clockwise. The structure is quite antique and, perhaps because of its neglected state, radiates a somewhat mournful air.

Typically, the stone-and-stucco structure has five distinct parts, each representing a sacred element. A squat square plinth, denoting earth, carries a four-stepped pyramid, water, widening upwards, as fire, to a truncated cone shape. Over that, a tall spire, air, culminates in a small disc, ether. In silhouette, the entirety recalls a seated figure in a pointed hat. Not really shrines but votive in their own right, chortens are an indication of monasteries nearby. The present ash-white example guards the approach to Lamayuru village.

The road forks. Straight ahead, uphill, is Lamayuru gompa, perched like an eyrie on the summit. The hill itself is clustered with smaller buildings, clinging like red-and-white beetles to its sides. The road branching to the right loops between some dwellings into a green valley of fields and trees. In this cold flat light, the place looks unnaturally static. It is almost 1 p.m.

A narrow dirt road is bisected by a long low wall of mani-stones with a whitewashed chorten at either end. I'm not entirely sure why we have turned onto it; we keep to the left of the manis.

The smooth flat stones, small and large, sienna and liver and mustard and grey, are incised with characters in Bodhi: *om mani padme hum*, ubiquitous mantra to Avalokiteshwara, Bodhisattva of Compassion, Lord-Protector of Travellers. On some of the stones, the six syllables of the chant are painted white, green, yellow, blue, red and black – each a panacea to pride, envy, desire, ignorance, possessiveness and hatred. This, I know, from early faddist leanings towards things Tibetan-Buddhist. At the far end of the wall, the road springs a nasty surprise of scree, tilting down into a boulder-filled ditch, far below, bordering some fields. The ground shifts under P.Singh – tentative, at first. I shut my eyes, hear ourselves ease into four-wheel drive. A deft three-point and, without damage to either automobile or antiquity, we are out of there, squeezing past the other side of the mani wall to where it began. We pause for breath, gather our wits, pop Polo mints and grin like asses. In a gully alongside, the main gates of a house are open wide.

The mascot of the Moonland Guesthouse is a black yak. The dreadlocked specimen stands in a sunken garden surrounded by little trees with pink and white blossoms that appear to be synthetic. But no; the apple trees are real, the bouquet of their inflorescence giddying the bees. It's the yak that is dead, mummified, its legs splayed like a trestle table and with glass bottles for eyes. Also on display are an ammonite-horned urial head, less well-endowed crania of other ovines and, in the branches of an apple, a mean-eyed hare with bared fangs. We aren't altogether bereft of human company. A monochromatic Ladakhi has been sorting a pile of water chestnuts on the garden steps. He seems studiously disinclined to acknowledge our presence. It is all rather strange. We turn to leave. A door flies open, releasing a figure like a jumpy marionette.

The young man, quite shoulderless, introduces himself with a nervous laugh as Sonam Something. Moonland had just reopened for the Season; if we planned to stay, we'd be their first guests. Rooms? Certainly; this way, please.

Our table at the edge of the garden overlooks fields of new barley and, for their backdrop, the hill with the gompa not far away. The mountains beyond are sunworshippers on a deserted beach. Here a tummy, there a face, pert breasts, hot pecs, firm butt, flabby thighs, crotch bulge, bellybutton, dimple, smile, hazily, lazily, deliciously erotic. We have lunched alfresco on noodle soup followed by stir-fried fresh veg and steamed rice. A flock of redstarts makes musical notes of themselves in the garden fence. The tablecloth attempts flight. Sonam reappears with cups of tea. I sugar mine and take it away with me.

My room has lavender walls and the bed, a slinky duvet of cerulean peonies. My neighbour's, peach walled, has a tiger-stripe duvet of similar slink. Both rooms have en suite bathrooms in incorruptible white. Our windows watch over taxidermy and apple trees.

7

The pencil is poised over a fresh page, waiting for the words to form themselves. It has been a day since the last entry. If I am to keep track of all that has slid into the realm of history, I'll be better off paring my scribbles to the essential details – rather like the stark but not bleak landscapes that have yielded them. Prayer flags. Child-monks. Gompa. Ignore the knock on the door and it will go away. Mani wheels. Lavender walls. Must be this thin air: the apple core by my side is slow to oxidize. Slinky duvet. The knocking on the door is sharper and insistent. I shut the notebook and go to see who has dared disturb my peace.

'Move it,' says Man. 'We're taking a walk to the monastery.'

'Later.'

'Now,' he says, wedging a foot between door and frame.

'Now,' parrots Sonam, bobbing up and down with a nervous grin. 'Please, sir. We must be there before three.'

Something tells me I'd be a fool not to accompany them.

The gompa stands literally up the road from Moonland but, as I am only just beginning to realise, the clear air and light has a trick of foreshortening distances. To reach the edifice has involved a stiff, mile-long trudge uphill.

The high whitewashed masonry walls are almost completely filled with ranges of glazed windows, trimmed in red and rising in diminishing tiers, all the way to the top of the complex. The walls themselves are tapered very slightly upwards to match the gradient of the rock hill. An elevated walkway along the outer perimeter has led, from full sun into afternoon shade, to the east-facing principal façade of the monastery.

Enclosed by the sun-worshipping mountains that we'd seen from Moonland, the floor of the valley seems to have sunk without warning to result in a deep crater, several miles wide. One half of it is in darkness, the other in light, its fissured yellow-orange sides flamed with shadows as though the rock were a vast tiger skin.

'There must have been a lake there,' I say almost to myself.

'Yes, sir,' says Sonam. 'Long time ago, which Guru Naropa made to vanish.'

'Vanish?'

It is a remarkable story, rendered that much more plausible by the conviction in its narrator's voice. Sometime during the eleventh century, an Indian Buddhist scholar, Guru Naropa, had spent years meditating inside a nearby cave, causing the lake to drain itself. Among the dregs was found a dead lion. It was taken as a sign by the Guru to raise a temple, which came to be known as Shenge Ghang, the Lion Mound. In time, Naropa's chief disciple Marpa had laid the foundations of the gompa in the shadow of which we are standing.

'I will show you the cave, sirs,' says Sonam, 'And also guru Naropa and Marpa, and guru Marpa's student Milarepa. We must go in now before the puja is finished.'

Dead lion. Cave. Puja. I have a dozen questions, but Sonam has taken off towards a stairway in the façade, leaving us to follow in perplexed silence.

It leads, through a modest doorway, into an inner courtyard, enclosed by verandas along three sides and, facing the main door, a raised gallery. The walls of the gallery are covered with murals in vivid chinoiserie. The red double-doors in the middle are embossed with bands of black and gold swastikas; a frilled canopy of multi-coloured silk is suspended above the lintel. The doors are padlocked at the threshold. A placard in a jamb informs Ladakh's oldest *dhukhang* – the gompa's assembly-hall – behind the doors. A closer look at the surrounding murals is thwarted by Sonam's urgency to get us up a stairway; a sonorous chanting has wafted briefly to the courtyard from somewhere upstairs.

We must remove our shoes before entering the chamber there. An eclectic mix of footwear is already parked outside.

In partial silhouette from the windows behind them, seven monks in maroon robes and red hats are seated side by side on thick floor-cushions. Before each monk is a low wooden table, cluttered with narrow sheaves of manuscript, a pair of brass cymbals, a little bell, Chinese teacups of grain (either wheat or barley) and, somewhat incongruously, packets of biscuits and boiled-sweets in shiny cellophane. Plenty of grain is spilled on the tables and the floor where the monks are seated.

In the middle of the chamber stands a large chorten, its sides piled high with hundreds of lumps of a brownish substance, roughly the size and shape of avocado pears. A range of carved and painted wooden cabinets along two walls is arranged with smaller chortens and gilded figures of Buddhist divinities. The murals behind them are streaked and faded; the wooden beams of the roof are hung with strips of brocade. Also present in the chamber is a group of lay people, seated on the floor and talking softly amongst themselves. Our entry seems to have coincided with a tea break.

One of the laity has poured each monk a cup of butter-tea from a large thermos patterned with florid red peonies. The monks sip and share a joke between themselves. The one in the middle acknowledges Sonam's bow of greeting with a nod and a smile. Our escort motions for us to sit, which we do, and then wedges himself between Man and me. Shortly, the monks set down their teacups and, to a synchronized flutter of cymbals, resume chanting from the manuscripts. Their voices are resonant – rising and falling in unison to a hypnotic cadence, trailing off, at the end of each verse and page, as barely audible rumbles. A clash of cymbals, and the cycle begins all over.

When the monks pause for another round of tea, I nudge Sonam: 'What's the significance?'

'For blessing the earth,' he whispers back. 'For a good season of sowing.'

So that explains the cups of grain. 'Is that wheat or barley?'

'Both.'

'And those ... things around the chorten?'

'Tsogs. Sacred offerings, made of tsampa and butter. Tsampa is barley flour. Mar, butter.'

Tsogs, I scribble into my notebook. And *tsampa* and *mar*.

'Write also,' says Sonam. 'Rinpoche. Head lama, there, in the middle. And this room is *lhakhang*. Temple.'

'The lion temple?'

'No. This is different.' Before he can elaborate, the monks launch into an energetic chorus, all the while taking up pinches of grain and scattering them to the four directions of the temple. The chants accelerate to a crescendo. At the same time, a young monk enters bearing a tray of flickering butter lamps which he places at the base of the central chorten. A resounding clash of cymbals and the proceedings come to an abrupt end.

If I've expected a Vajrayana Buddhist prayer service to be a grim solemn affair, my first experience of one has been a delightful surprise, not least for the laid-back air of the principal participants. The monks have removed their red hats and sat back to sip more tea and laugh and chat. One by one, the members of the laity step up to gift the Rinpoche a narrow white scarf which he, in turn, drapes around their neck. Some of the others, meanwhile, start to disassemble the mountain of tsogs, collecting the objects in conical willow baskets like backpacks with headstraps that are hoisted up and taken away; those, says Sonam, will be distributed in the village. The monks prepare to leave, wrapping the manuscripts in lengths of red fabric and tucking away their teacups inside the folds of their robes. Everyone stands aside, bowing low as the Rinpoche and the monks exit the temple. After they've left, one of the women hands around the tsogs remaindered at the base of the chorten.

'Eat,' she says. 'Good for health.'

Sonam is already nibbling on his. Man and I sample a pinch and decide this is definitely an acquired taste; the woman and Sonam exchange an amused jabber of Ladakhi. Bloody fools, they seem to be saying. With that, we leave the temple and return downstairs.

That the gompa of Lamayuru belongs to the Drigung-pa sub-sect of the Kagyu-pa 'red-hat' order (the other order being the Gelugs-pa 'yellow-hat') has been established a short while ago. One of the monks has stayed behind in the courtyard to see off the laity. Sonam goes up to ask if we may be permitted to visit the dhukhang behind the red doors. Waiting for the monk to fetch the key, he provides an introduction to the figures in the murals of the gallery.

The Four Guardians of the Quarters are represented as celestial warlords in wildly swirled robes, auras of billowing flames and clouds framing their crowned visages. Kubera, Guardian of the North, is yellow of complexion and holds a pennant in his right hand and a mongoose in his left. Vimdhaka, blue Guardian of the South, wields a double-edged sword in each hand. To the right of the door is Virupaksha, hot-red Guardian of the West, clutching a writhing serpent in his right hand and, in the left, a chorten to his chest. The corresponding figure to the left is Dhritarashtra, peachy Guardian of the East and the friendliest of the lot, playing a lute. Each divinity is accompanied by a crouching attendant, gazing adoringly up.

The space over the figures is worked as a trompe l'oeil of embroidered silk frills; the motif is continued in the adjacent walls of the gallery.

The mural on the left-hand side wall is a history of the gompa, annotated in minuscule Bodhi script and rendered as a continuous-narrative of scenic cameos in which a monk – presumably Guru Naropa or Guru Marpa; Sonam isn't sure – is seated in meditation surrounded by lotuses, moves on to meditate in a chamber of some sort, appears in conversation with lay people, receives a grandee at the entrance of a gompa – presumably this very gompa – and stands in a posture of worship at the red doorway of a courtyard – presumably this very courtyard. Integrated into the mural is an actual door in the wall, giving onto a warren of chambers and another flight of steps, all of which, Sonam indicates, are off limits. So we turn from the history mural to look at the opposite wall.

The mural there is a representation of a *Kalachakra*, the Wheel of Time from which all sentient beings must strive, over countless rebirths, to break free in order to attain that elusive Shangri-La, *nirvana*. The wheel itself is wrought as three concentric circles filled with itsy-bitsy symbols which leave its current, uninitiated viewers more than a little befuddled. Sonam commences a commentary but is interrupted by the return of the monk with the key. Ushering us through the ornate red doors, he pulls them shut on Man, Sonam and me.

The large square hall is filled with southern light, streaming in from the windows to the left. From the rows of low tables to the tall wooden columns, the runners between the aisles to the window frames, the divans along the tables to the banners in the rafters, everything in the hall is articulated in a scheme of red, with accents of gold, yellow, blue and green. The entire length of the wall to the right is occupied by a glass-fronted cabinet, filled with hundreds, possibly thousands, of manuscripts wrapped in red fabric. An altar at the far end of the central aisle carries a life-size image of a Buddhist divinity, flanked by smaller figures of Buddhas, and portraits of the Dalai Lama and the gompa's Rinpoches, present and past. A little below the altar is a cushioned platform like a throne, no doubt for the use of the incumbent Rinpoche.

We've paused, beside the altar, at a glass case containing an enormous chorten. The structure appears to be of carved wood, with painted silver and gold details. But no. A placard indicates the structure was moulded from yakbutter in 1975; the one in the temple upstairs is a more antique counterpart.

A door behind the display has led us into a long low chamber. Below a window by the door are a number of butter lamps, all of them lit. It is an odd effect: the little flames licking the afternoon light spilling onto them. But that's not the only thing odd about the room.

If something sits in the same spot long enough, it tends to charge the air around it with a palpable energy. The icons in a glass case along one wall clearly haven't budged in centuries. The force radiating from them is as compelling as it is repellent; we seem to have stepped into the spiritual and mystical core of the gompa. I stay long enough to note the Twenty-One Taras, seated in a row beneath the larger, wrathful glassed-in divinities.

Among the offerings of plastic flowers, wax fruit and currency notes piled about the bases of the images is a plastic and faux-fur menagerie of beasties, endemic and non-endemic. I turn for an explanation only to find myself quite alone in the chamber. Time to scoot.

Outside in the assembly hall, a niche between the stacks of manuscripts is fronted by glazing, splotched with marks where foreheads have pressed between hands to peer in. Through the glass darkly are three life-size images, seated together in a tunnel-like cavity. One of the figures is more realistic than its companion pair. I feel a goose dance all over my grave.

'Cave,' says Sonam. 'Guru Naropa. Guru Marpa. Guru Milarepa. Forever meditating.'

A passage like a tunnel along the southern extremity of the gompa has opened onto a terrace in the western prospect. A collection of towering chortens here are brilliantly colour-washed and adorned with stucco mouldings of prancing lions. At waist-height in the west-face of the gompa's basement and continuing along the plinths of the chortens, a shallow niche is filled with hundreds of cylindrical prayer wheels, the embossed Bodhi characters on their sides spelling *om mani padme hum* in crimson on white. Sonam leads, trundling the manis with his right hand; we follow close behind, doing the same, all the better to accumulate karmic merit.

Where the terrace ends, the ground falls away as a confusion of flat uneven rooftops, with glimpses of narrow pathways zigzagging in between. Sonam has skipped down some rough-hewn stone steps and, rather than keep to a cobbled path there, scampers along a dirt track to the left. It brings us to the base of the looming masonry foundations of the gompa crowning the hill.

The lower slope is blistered with closely packed mud-brick dwellings which seem to have sprouted, organically, from the bare rock surfaces with little concern for either the principles of architecture or the rules of gravity. The effect is that of a termite mound turned inside out, and one that the residents have long since evacuated. The dirt track suddenly tilts as a stretch of scree angled sharply downhill – mind your step – towards a small square. A tarchen there is frayed to grey threads. The façades enclosing the square are riddled with windows with broken glazing and shutters hanging from their hinges. The sense of bleakness is overpowering.

'What is this place?' I ask our young friend.

'The old village, sir,' Sonam replies. 'That house was where my grandfather used to live. And that one there, the grandparents of my best friend. Something happened and everyone left.'

'Something?'

'I don't know, sir. It was a very long time ago.'

'Where did everyone go?'

'To the other side of the hill, sir, to where we are going. But first I must show you Shenge Ghang.'

It appears that the sole purpose of making our way through the abandoned village has been to take in the Lion Mound shrine. We arrive at it via a maze of alleys, not once encountering a soul along the way. The faded red doors in the crumpled mud-brick wall are locked. Sonam runs a hand over the lintel, is visibly disappointed to find the key missing.

'If you will wait, sirs, I will go find it.'

'Don't worry,' says Man quickly. 'We can see it another time.'

'Yes, absolutely,' I agree. Somehow, it's enough to stand outside Guru Naropa's lion shrine and imagine what it must contain. Aside from which, I could do with a strong shot of caffeine.

The new village, thereafter, is announced by a low gateway surmounted by a chorten. The houses on this side are decidedly lived-in, with tarchoks in their roof ridges and potted geraniums in window sills. The gravity-defying quality of the architecture endures in these bare rock faces. Some houses are wedged, like mad birds' nests, into the fissures in the hillside and accessed by narrow bridges between one rock ledge and the next. All the façades overhang the valley through which the Indus flows broad and swift.

My pencil is poised over a fresh page, waiting for the words that must follow *Moonland 6 p.m.*

When there are none forthcoming, I shut the notebook. The mountains behind the crater have turned into a single undulating mass of mauve. In the façade of the gompa, little rectangles of amber start to come on tier by tier. The houses on the hill soon follow suit. The sky has gone from powder blue to salmon.

'Your little book,' says Man, apropos of nothing. 'Material for the next undertaking?'

'Not really. There's still the other thing to wrap up.'

'You're going to abandon it anyway.'

I don't recall saying or doing anything to substantiate the assumption. 'I am?'

An uneasy silence, to fill which I reopen the notebook. *Lights like fireflies to jewelbox. M of opinion will chuck TL. Totally inaccurate. Will see through to completion come what may.*

'Right.' says Man, stretching hugely. 'See you at dinner.'

8

5.50 a.m. The water in the washbasin is jaw-numbingly cold. I hear footfalls in the passage, followed by a soft knock on the door. It is Sonam, with a bucket of hot water. I thank him and dive back into the bathroom. In three minutes flat, I'm done and partially dried, also colder than I was before. Shaking out the clothes that have spent the night on the hook, I send yesterday's smalls flying into a puddle. To hell; I stick them back on the hook and pull on my jeans and sweatshirt.

6.30 a.m. We're through with breakfast, cleared our bill and set to leave. Sonam asks if he can hitch a ride to Leh. If that's fine with us, he'll just take a minute to grab a bag. Of course it is fine. I dash back to the rooms, meanwhile, to check if we've left anything behind, retrieve my almost-dry almost-forgottens and shove them into a pocket.

Man and Sonam are already in P.Singh. 'Is everything alright?'

'Brilliant,' I reply and fasten my seatbelt.

The 'moonland' landscape, viewed yesterday from the gompa walkway, is spectacular up close and in the morning light. That the crater was indeed a lake is suggested by ossified tidemarks on the sulphur-yellow rock sides. The bottom is riddled with gigantic cones and funnels, remaindered after the water had gone wooshing through into nothing. The effect is that of a gigantic old egg tray.

'Sonam, what's the Ladakhi word for egg?'

'*Thul*, sir.'

'Thul. That's easy to remember. And what would you call an egg tray?'

'Ah, we call it egg tray, sir.'

A shaggy mountain dog is seated by the road. 'And those?' asks Man.

'*Zhankey*, sir.'

I ought to be taking notes but it is less pedantic to memorize the words as they pop up as captions to the passing sights.

'That?' Man points to a cairn of stones crowned in twigs and prayer flags.

'No, sir,' Sonam corrects me; *that* is not a chorten. The name for it is *lha tho*. Note the pronunciation or confusion may occur. La*h* tho, whereas la is mountain-pass and tso is lake (that's something we already know). The word for any mountain is *ri* and its peak, *rigo*. A river – like this one, the Indus – is *chu*. Those sheep and goats bleating their way down to the water, also chu, are, collectively, *ralug*. The generic term for a village is *yul* and the unisex gowns worn by these *yulpa* are *goncha*. The turquoise-and-coral studded hat that *abi*, grandmother, has on is a *perak*. That old man reminds Sonam of his *meme*, grandfather. That house is big, which makes it a *khang chen*; that one, small, is *khang bu*. Look! There beside that *drimo*, cow-yak, a magpie, *katangputit*, is teasing a *phia*, marmot. And now a zhankey has joined the *chipa*, bird. Fantastic.

'How old are you, Sonam?'

'Seventeen, sir. How old are you, sir?'

'Seventeen too. Now stop calling me sir.'

'You look older, sir.' Cheeky bugger. 'Are you married, sir?'

'No, Sonam, I am not. But this meme is.' The meme growls. 'And he has two sons, one of whom is a little younger than us. Are you married?'

'I will marry when I am twenty-two.'

'Tell us about Ladakhi weddings, Sonam.'

'There are many ceremonies, sirs. Three days, sometimes four. First in my house, then in my … her house, then I go to her house and then she comes to my house and then we go together to her house, then we both come back to my house when we are properly married. Many prayers and a big party with many different foods and *chang*.'

I haven't heard that word since Tintin. 'Brilliant. Does chang taste good?'

'Very good, sir.'

'Have you ever seen a yeti, Sonam?'

'No, sir. There is no yeti in Lamayuru. I once saw a *tenmo* in Zanskar. I wish very much to see a *shan*, but it is rare.'

'Do you like animals?'

'Very much, sir. I also like history and geography. I like to read. In Leh, I always go to the public library first.'

Turns out he's through with high-school finals and awaiting his results. If all goes well, he'll attempt the National Defence Academy selections. I'm not entirely sure about that, considering his skinny frame. This thought I keep to myself.

8.45 a.m. We've been coursing minus subtitles for a bit. The river to the right is calm as a python and the breeze through the windows, equally languid. A short way past Lardo village, the opposite bank presents a clutch of houses, nestled between a stretch of poplars. There are no signs of activity there or down by the river. A ropeway across the water looks inviting. Synchronous thoughts: we pull up by the side.

It is a pukka affair, composed of parallel steel cables stretched between squat masonry towers on either bank. A small, metal-frame trolley is suspended over the water. Two lengths of sturdy burlap tape, passed over flywheels, are tied from the sides of the trolley to the corresponding towers. The mechanism is foolproof: pull one or the other tape to convey the trolley forth or back. Three is a crowd; Sonam offers to stay.

The contraption is a breeze to manoeuvre. All I have to do is pull. We are both seated on the wooden floor of the trolley with our legs through the metal-frame sides. Three-quarters of the way along the roughly 200-feet cables, an inexplicable snag brings the wretched thing to a stop. A smart yank at the tape only makes matters worse; tugging the one on Man's side makes no difference. Sonam is not where he had waved us off. There's still no movement around the ostensibly inhabited houses. The breeze is delighted to dissolve our shouts. There's nothing for it but to sit this out, so we wait, back-to-back, some fifty feet over the Indus.

I find it hard to reel in my eyes from the water. Café au lait, it is adrift with bits and bobs of chocolate deadwood. It must be deep and freezing cold. The trolley rocks ever so gently in each passing draught. We could be dangling here forever. My thoughts go into overdrive. We could, of course, swim back to shore, unless, of course, that too goes wrong. Cold-shock aside, our layers and boots will bog us down in no time at all. In which case, it might be wiser to undress and jump off and retrieve this lot, somehow, after we've towelled down. Unless I'm very much mistaken, P.Singh was locked, which would mean the keys are on Man.

'Random question. Are P's keys on you?'

'Yes.'

'Clipped to your belt loop and tucked into your pocket? NO *don't move.*'

'Yes. Relax.'

Must think this through before suggesting the plunge. Must both of us go? What if one or the other accidentally lets the keys drown. Where is the spare? What if Sonam cannot be found, if no one else is using the deserted road, if those houses are in fact abandoned, the tape on Man's side *somehow* gets cut, the sky darkens, the breeze turns to wind, the temperature drops, the cold steel cables serrate our palms, they are too well greased anyway to grapple across like Bruce or Tom, so we are stuck in the trolley and compelled to risk starvation dehydration hypothermia desiccation or strip down to essentials and risk freezing our –

'*Bollocks!* Of all bloody days.'

'What now?'

'Nothing. How are you doing?'

'Fine. Great views from up here.'

'Spectacular.'

'Good. There's Sonam.'

The stick-figure has scampered down to the towers to sit in their shadow. We wave to catch his attention; he waves back. He's too far to hear us; perhaps he thinks we've stopped for a breath. Damn. But bingo! I squirm for my pocket and yank out the bulge, causing the trolley to violently rock. 'What the – ' Man frowns, turning around; if only he could see his own expression. Everything happens for a very good reason. I flag out my nifty red smalls.

Sonam gets to his feet. Man and I are flailing our arms now, he miming pull-us-to-shore. For all this jiggling, it's a wonder the trolley doesn't tip us over. Sonam is quick to assess what's happened. His wire-thin frame must be tough as titanium. Wedging himself against the masonry tower, he gives the tape a sharp tug. Something gives and the trolley lurches. With no help from us, Sonam starts to pull, not letting the tape even for a moment slacken. He is quite winded but laughing when we tumble out. He'd been sitting behind the towers all along – and an eye on P.Singh soaking in the sun.

This place ought to carry a large red signboard: *FOOLS KEEP OUT*.

Alchi, 10.45 a.m. We've taken a diversion off the highway to visit a group of early Vajrayana Buddhist temples. Going by the signboards along the road, Alchi claims Model Village status in addition to that of a Heritage Site. It is set, prettily, in a valley of mustard fields, apricot and poplar, through which the Indus makes a loop. Guarding the approach are three new-looking chortens, painted yellow, white and blue. We are waved on by elders in trad, sitting at the doorsteps of trad houses; something feels a tad put-on, a bit too eager to look genuine. The village itself is a vehicle-free zone. We leave P.Singh in the company of a grocer's near the bus stop.

Sonam is eager to show us around. By his own admission, he has nothing pressing to do in Leh, so long as he can get there by dusk. Everyone in the village square seems to know him; plenty of julleys fly to and fro as he leads the way down a cobbled path.

It winds between masonry walls that have recently received a lick of whitewash. Peering over the copings are branches laden with tiny green fruit; the raw apricots are piquant. A door in the right-hand side wall gives into the grounds of a modern hotel in a studiedly understated vernacular idiom. A corresponding door, to the left, opens onto an alfresco restaurant with a fawning manager and no customers. Further down the path, an intersection with a small mani shrine under a tree is watched over by a clutch of lopsided streethouses, all of them whitewashed and with gingham half-curtains. The windows of a souvenir shop are displayed with Buddhist sculptures and thangkas; on the doorstep, an abi in costume is saying her prayer beads with a mobile pressed to her ear. The path turns where three crumbling chortens occupy a corner. A door in the wall beside them is shut. We keep to the path.

It runs parallel, now, to a high straight wall. Downhill, to our left, a gully of trees and cultivation has a wedge of mountains for its backdrop. Another turn presents a view of the Indus and, across it in the distance, a large metal bridge the colour of rust. In the wall beside us, a low doorway is open. It is the entrance to the Heritage Site. I leave my cynicism at the door and duck through behind Sonam and Man into a long passage.

The whole of its right side is a long mani-wall – the prayer wheels framed in red woodwork and reflecting the sun in warm gold-brass. Three right-hands, one following the other, turn each mani as we slowly walk past. Their collective trundle grows into a sonorous hum which puts me in an inordinately mellow mood. The embossed mantras shimmer, over and over, and then fall silent, one by one. At the end of the range, a solitary mani occupies a cloister of its own. This one is large and painted red, green and blue, its calligraphic mantra illuminated in gold. A hidden bell chimes when the mani is turned.

The passage has flowed seamlessly into a courtyard dotted with apricot trees and several low white-stucco structures. A monk in maroon greets Sonam with great familiarity and us with a vague smile of welcome. There is a small donation to be made here: *Received with thanks the sum of rupees thirty only for the Restoration of Alchi Chhoskhor Temple*. Hanging from a tree is a hand-painted sign.

ATTENTION PLEASE

1. Photography is strickly prohibited in-side the temples.
2. Smoking & consuming alcoholik drinks in the vicinity of the temples also strickly prohibited.
3. Please cooperate with the management to keep the environment of the temples neat and clean.

Sonam has removed his shoes under the tree. I park mine next to his. Suddenly liberated of lace-ups and socks, my feet feel wonderful on the warm cobblestones. There is no specific route in which the monuments must be taken; we leave it to the monk and Sonam to guide us around. The former provides a historical framework in English with a vaguely French accent.

Established in the eleventh century, around the same time as the revival of Buddhism in Tibet and the founding of the gompa in Lamayuru, Alchi had flourished for close to three hundred years before, for reasons unknown, active worship at the temples had ceased during the sixteenth century. Spared, therefore, the attendant wear and tear of continued use, and thanks in equal measure to the arid conditions of their setting, the temples' contents of Vajrayana iconography, painted and sculptural, had only slightly weathered. The dhukhang and a *sumstek* (three-storey) temple, both dating from the late eleventh century, were found to contain the finest and best-preserved works.

We have stopped beside a white stucco structure crowned with two chortens. Beckoning us closer to the structure, the monk motions for us to look inside.

A doorway leads into a narrow chamber with a small chorten in the middle. Seated there is a visitor from a foreign land, gazing up. She tears her eyes away to acknowledge us with a little nod and exits through a different door in the opposite wall. We enter, and occupy the same spot.

The sides of the chorten have faded paintings of sacred symbols, lotus foliation and horses bearing parasols but no riders. Directly above, the vaulted ceiling of the chamber – it is the inner surface of the chorten crowning the structure – tapers up as a series of diminishing squares tipped on their axes.

Every inch of the vaulting is covered with intricate paintings in a still-vibrant palette of cobalt and vermilion, with figural details in black, white and ochre. Thousands of little Buddhas, seated in meditation, occupy auras organized in neat rows and columns. Flying celestials and winged oxen are interspersed with elaborate bands of rosettes and *vajras*. The brushwork is remarkably precise. The light from the doorways lends the painted surfaces a subtle, third dimension, at once reminiscent of fine flock wallpaper. It crosses my mind that the murals may have been worked as flat sections on prepared fabric-ground and then pasted onto the stucco surfaces; some facets of the vaulting couldn't possibly have been reached by a brush. Whatever the techniques of their forgotten artisans, the effects are a mere foretaste of the temples-proper.

A maze of passages and doorways has brought us into the forecourt of the dhukhang. A surprise garden here, enclosed by disused rooms for monks, is thriving with poppies and irises and a rambling rose drenched in pink blooms. The architecture itself is a series of transitions, literal and metaphoric, from sunlit areas through darkness into illumination.

Accessed by a nondescript doorway, the assembly-hall is a square inner courtyard surrounded by loggias. The carved and painted wooden columns everywhere have sprung rampant lions and fabulous hybrid creatures. Deep in shadows, the rear walls carry floor-to-ceiling murals in muted primary colours. The themes are predominantly sacred. Beyond the Four Guardians of the Quarters, I am completely at sea before the larger pantheon of Vajrayana divinities. More intriguing are the smaller, secular themes sharing the same wall surfaces: whimsical little landscapes and buildings; lay people engaged in mundane chores; stylized yet recognizable plants, birds and animals.

To one side of the courtyard and under a glass case is a Kalachakra *mandala*, laid out in multi-coloured sands. This one is purely for display, remarks the monk; its symbolisms haven't been infused with sacred powers.

There's no dearth of powers to the icons in alcoves flanking the door of the main shrine-chamber. The gilded and painted plaster Bodhisattvas are festooned in offerings of prayer beads, paper money and *kata* scarves. The fine dust covering the images serves, paradoxically, only to heighten their strange aura of realism.

The shrine is dedicated to the Five Wisdom Buddhas. Looming from the half-light on a pedestal in the middle, a lifelike seated figure of Mahavairocana, the Great Illuminator, clutches the Wheel of Dhamma and his consort, the White Tara. Surrounding the central pair and aligned to the cardinal directions are the associated Wisdoms and their female counterparts. To the east sit Akshobya and Locana: blue, touching the earth and representing spring. Amitabha and Pandara: red, west, meditating, summer. Ratnasambhava and Mamaki: yellow, south, munificent, autumn. Amogasiddhi and Green Tara: green, north, fearless, winter.

The groupings are sheltered by a large Tree of Enlightenment, also of painted plaster, frenetic with elephants, celestial dancers, musicians and mythical creatures. It is all very intriguing and wildly baroque, too clustered with obscure symbolisms to take in at one go. I am seized, not for the first time, by a weird sensation that the figures will, any moment, shift their gazes and gestures. I turn away to look at the shadowy walls.

The surfaces are entirely worked as elaborate mandalas – two-dimensional representations of the Wisdom Buddhas and the Thousand Meditating Buddhas – with cameos in between of daily life and ritual. The scenes here are luxuriously detailed, as though their painters had all the time in the world to lavish this level of jewel-like perfection. I am riveted by a bird, the size of an open palm, adorning a corner of one of the mandalas. Some ten centuries after it has been rendered, its fabulous plumage still holds its iridescence. When all is shuttered up and quiet at night, it must surely chirrup and fly around in circles.

The neighbouring courtyard is dappled in the shadows of gnarled old apricots. Two small, square temples here share a common wall. The Lotswa, literally 'translator', Lhakhang commemorates a twelfth-century Tibetan Buddhist scholar, Rinchen Zangpo. The murals in the shrine are understated to the point of being austere. The ravages of time are more evident; some haphazard attempts at restoration have left a section of artwork incongruously brighter than its immediate surrounds. The monk draws our attention to a painted portrait of the Great Translator. The youthful figure is depicted in lotus-pose, beatifically smiling and framed in concentric auras.

The adjoining Manjushri Lhakhang, late twelfth century, is eponymous. Here, a vividly-coloured image of the sword-bearing Bodhisattva of Truth is surrounded by crumbling murals. More sculptures and paintings are ranged behind glass in a cloister at the rear. The dank interiors are suffocatingly oppressive. I can do without making a thorough tour; the air under the trees is deliciously cool.

We are back near the chortens in the main courtyard. There is one more temple that our companions are keen to show us. Something in their manner suggests they have saved the sumstek for last.

The principal façade of the three-storeyed temple is exuberant with carved woodwork, expressed through the levels as columns and balconies, projected eaves, leaping-lion brackets, foliated architraves, fretworked panels, turned pendant finials, lotus medallions and, over the entrance porch, delicate little Buddhas in pierced trefoil cartouches. The sun has sucked out much of the colour from the Four Guardians in the entrance porch. Directly over the doorway, a fearsome blue Mahakala prances across a grinning cadaver. Be still, my beating heart. We step through.

It is a square chamber, the light filtering in from the door and the tiered galleries above. In the middle, a decorated chorten on a stepped base is surrounded by four carved wooden columns supporting beams enriched with Buddhas, foliated scrollwork and brocade banners. I move clockwise around the central feature, allowing my eyes to adjust to the dim interior.

The murals are more opulent than any at the other temples, their colours more concentrated, vivid and almost luminous. The walls, moreover, are incorporated with wide, double-height niches. There are three niches in all. Standing in each is an enormous plaster sculpture.

Only the limbs and torsos of the figures are visible, and when I lean forward and peer up, their chests, shoulders and crowned visages guarding the topmost level of the interior. The Bodhisattvas are breathtakingly beautiful, with inscrutable half-smiles to their faces. Each divinity is dressed, from waist to the knees, in dhoti-like garments which at first glance appear to be of embroidered cloth. They are not; the plasterwork drapery is integral to the sculptures and exquisitely decorated with painted miniatures.

Avalokiteshwara, white Bodhisattva of Compassion, in the niche in the west-wall, is clothed in a tapestry of minute palaces and temples. Garlands and ornaments about his neck, chest and torso are picked out in gold and jewel colours. The niche in the north houses Maitreya, the golden Future Buddha. His garment is painted with scenes from the life of the Buddha, described in medallions. Jade-green and sword-bearing, Manjushri, in the east-niche, is adorned with the Eighty-five Masters of the Tantra, seated in checkerboard-like mandalas. The temple is no longer in use, yet draped from the fingers of the divinities and placed at their feet are assorted offerings from the devout. Katas, coins and rupee notes, little strings of prayer beads, a sprig of apple blossom, the odd plastic trinket, a windup wristwatch – litanies, wishes, hopes and gratitude – all left undisturbed and gathering dust.

The upper levels of the temple are off bounds to visitors. I lose count of my circumabulations, in the ground floor, of the central chorten. The others have stepped outside some time ago. There is no reason for me to not linger before the monumental Saviours, each time finding a new detail to look at.

A draught touches the banners and accoutrements, awakens hints of old incense held in by the walls. A slant of light spangles the suspended dust. If this were the last temple I visit in these parts, the image I must forever treasure is of the great eyes of the Bodhisattvas, gazing serenely outwards. They'll probably exchange broad winks after I'm gone.

2.40 p.m. We are the only guests at the alfresco restaurant. Lunch is a somewhat rich fare of curried vegetables and pilaf. Sonam is neither surprized nor inconvenienced by an impulsive change in our schedule: we have decided to stay the night at the hotel across the cobbled path. He assures us there are any number of buses plying between Alchi and Leh; he must leave at once in order to catch one; no, sirs, please don't come to see me off. We bid julleys at the door of the restaurant with hugs and exchanges of addresses, and hopes that our paths will once again cross.

With Sonam gone, a familiar silence settles across the table. The afternoon is stretched languidly ahead. It should be interesting to set out, a little later, on solo tramps.

9

Someone else has had the same idea for the afternoon and beaten me to the metal bridge. It's the woman from the chortens this morning. Her legs are dangled over the edge. She is buried in a book, an apple in the other hand. Apple; bridge. I'm reminded of something.

Driving back to Lucknow from Lakhimpur Kheri with my dear old friend 'Papa' John Wakefield from a visit to his buddy of half a century, Dudhwa National Park's Billy Arjan Singh, we had been stuck, on a similar bridge, behind a lorry loaded with crates of apples. Few things in life can be more torturous than the scent of something you cannot quite have. This had been excruciating. The ultimate apple-junkie, unable to sate my thing for the original Fruit of Sin; the driver of the lorry, bastard, refusing to give me a dozen of his shipment. Woe is me, once again. The cores of the last of Man's and my cache were consigned, last night, to the base of a flowering Lamayuru apple tree.

Random connections have brought me directly behind Eve of The Bridge. She squints up, shielding her face from the sun with the book in her hand. It is *too* much of a coincidence, even for me. *Honorary Tiger*, Billy's biography by Duff Hart-Davis. I must look the perfect creep, grinning down. Her expressions change like water from smile of recognition to frown of enquiry to scowl of outright annoyance.

'Excuse me?'

'I've met him. Arjan Singh.' How gauche it must sound.

'Yeah right.'

'In fact, I reviewed the book ... Look, I'm sorry. Didn't mean to disturb or anything.'

'Really?' She puts Duff face-down by her side, takes another crunch at her waxed-perfect Washington Red and comes back with a rather limp challenge. 'What's it about, then?'

'A tigress called Tara, deer called barasingha, and a nonagenarian with deep blue eyes and thunderous voice. Loved it all. See you around.'

'Hang on. Did you meet him recently?'

'Last December.'

'They told me he wasn't there last week.'

Interesting. 'Where did you look?'

'They said he no longer lived in Tiger Haven.'

'Should've looked harder. He's in his other haven nearby.'

'And you met him there? In this other place?'

'A full fabulous week.'

She calls up her legs and sits hugging them. 'Awesome. I did see one tiger, but it was shy. And some rhino inside the electric fence forest. Is he ... *nice*?'

'Everything that the book makes him out to be. And more.'

'Hey, care for an apple?'

'Oh! Thanks.' She has a whole stash in her daypack.

'Welcome. So tell me. What … is he like? As a person.'

'Delightful. What more can I say.'

I have no intention of repeating Billy's warning to me to *not* visit the Rana Tharu hamlets on the Indo-Nepal border. 'Do *not* … go *there*,' he had bellowed one morning, 'the *women* … will *cast* … the … *evil* eye … on *you*.'(I'd gone, of course, and returned with two tinkling cowbells.) Or mentioning the doggy-graves in his garden and the yellow mustard fields, the giant Devil's Tree guarding the bungalow and the battered typewriter in the front veranda, the red-woollen elf-cap and the long-idle barbells, ancestors on mantelpieces, log-fires roaring, ingratiating old retainers, chilled stewed apples for breakfast, fine Darjeeling through the day. And Billy declaiming Kipling, full blast, tears streaming, on the back veranda our last morning:

What of the hunting, hunter bold?
Brother, the watch was long and cold.
What of the quarry ye went to kill?
Brother, he crops in the jungle still.
Where is the power that made your pride?
Brother, it ebbs from my flank and side.
Where is the haste that ye hurry by?
Brother, I go to my lair to die!

'Write … *that* … in your … *next* book,' he had commanded, settling back in his chair. An hour later, 'Papa' and our driver and I had trailed the apple-crate lorry.

Tempus fugit. I fish out the baby apricots in my pockets from a tree at the hotel. 'Try some?'

She selects one. 'What are they?'

Never pass up a chance to name drop. '*Prunus armeniaca*. Edible also in baby form, as I have only recently discovered.'

'Hmm. Tart.' She helps herself to another. 'Apricot.'

'Yep.' The view from the bridge of the opposite bank doesn't look especially inviting for a snoop. Just a bare wall of mountain and the detritus of some road-building works. 'I think I'll head back and keep to this side. Thanks again for the apple.'

'Ciao.'

Down by the water, the Indus is a loud cold sheet of milky opal. The shore is pebbled in every conceivable hue on earth, from darkest grape to marzipan. The pebbles are coolly smooth in my palm.

I am struck, yet again, by how effortlessly the pictures change and with little intimation, if at all.

There are no pebbles along this stretch of the riverbank, barely a mile downstream. I've found my way here through the village. A bridle path – below the cobbled one to the chhoskhor – has skittered down the gully into a brooding stand of willows and apricot. The sound of water has steadily amplified. The trees stay back; the ground is taken over by grasses. Low drystone walls, marking the sides of individual acres, wend their way to, and right into, the river. When in spate, the Indus must rise to the treeline; plastic bottles and mismatched shoes lie half-buried in the grass. A broken red jerrycan has sprouted a festival of yellow daisies. A lone rose bush, taller than myself, is lightly shrugging off its surplus pink petals. The sheer wall of mountain across the river is rust. Away to the right, a corner of the metal bridge is just visible, with a far crest of snow peaks completing the composition. To the left, the Indus curves and disappears between geological architecture. Flapping high above the flow, a furlong of prayer flags bridges the ramparts.

The village is silent. A narrow alley between the dwellings has opened onto a puddle of sun. To one side, a flock of dinky pashminas are penned behind a woven-wire fence. The goats are friendly; they also have a nifty nip. By the side of the fence is a young black yak – alive, not stuffed. With their backs to the yak are five seated figures. They turn and size up the intrusion.

The first four women are dressed to the hilt like superannuated divas awaiting a curtain call. Each has on a tall satin hat, the brims scrolling up the sides of their crinkled-fruit faces. Their hair is done in pigtails finished in shiny bows. Embroidered mint and cherry silk *bok*s cut swish complements to the backs of their coffee and plum velvet gonchas. The fifth woman, Renoiresque in complexion and proportions, is less splendidly attired: black bomber jacket, scarlet headscarf and salwaar. Sitting behind the party is a half-empty liquor bottle of a cloudy brew, a baby-feeding bottle (half-full of something non-lactic from its hue), and a blue-and-white plastic Vaseline jar. The biddies say something to their peachy companion. She hurrumphs and swivels right around. An infant in her ample arms is itself enormous and packaged in many-coloured woollens.

'*Ay*, tooris,' the woman calls. Her voice is a rasp. I ignore her, making an elaborate show of befriending the yak.

'*Ay*, tooris,' she repeats, forcefully. 'Take foto.'

'No foto, thank you. Julley blah blah.'

The duchesses cackle and say something more, at which their fecund front promptly shoves Piggy down and thrusts up for my view what appears, at first, to be an exceptionally large muskmelon. It is oily-yellow, with a wetly mangled mulberry teat. Still yielding forward the wobbly mass, the gorgon makes a disagreeable rubbing gesture with her free thumb and forefinger.

'Take foto. Give rupis.'

Just my freakish bloody luck. Trot, I tell myself and do just that.

The door of our room is ajar. 'An odd thing just happened,' I begin and stop.

Man is flat out, staring at the ceiling, hands pressed to his temples. He looks a bit green. 'Are you alright?'

'No.'

'Oh. As in … what?'

'I don't know.'

'That doesn't help very much. Head? Stomach? Toppley? Vomitous?'

He glowers up, no doubt attempting a 'fierce' expression. '*I-will-be-fine*, okay? Must be something we ate. Anyway. How was your walk.'

'Fruitful. And yours?'

'Terrific.'

'I ran into some women.'

'So did I.'

'Lucky us. With goats and a yak, by any chance?'

'No. In a field. Two trekkers.'

That safely rules out any evil-eye juju (to which I am anyway immune). To alleviate his grump, I furnish a description of the Muskmelon, complete with accent and actions. It works.

'You are sick,' he says, dashing for the loo.

10

It is a remarkably featureless stretch of flat road, the sides coursing aridly to merge, miles away, with the surrounding drab slopes. Tracks in the friable earth bear evidence of a popular motoring activity known as 'off-roading'. A speck of colour in the monotony grows into a blue and yellow shrine on the left hand side. Pointing at it from the driver's side, a small signboard reads *Cannonbal Mandir*. A larger board carries the legend *Magnetic Hill The Phenomenon That Defies Gravity Park Your Vehicle In The Box Marked With White Paint On The Road* with a tiny rectangle and downward-pointing arrow. There's nothing to be seen on the even tarred surface; we've probably stopped directly over said mark.

'Hang on, don't reverse. We must be directly over – '

'I'm not reversing.'

'Yes you are.'

'I am *not*.' Odd. His feet are off all pedals and the gearshift is in neutral.

'Then why the – '

'Weeeeeeeeeeeeeeeeeee!'

Whether we like it or not, all two-something tonnes of us is moving backwards, *uphill*, and very fast. Courtesy perspective, the signboards and the shrine are rapidly diminishing into the foreground. We've covered maybe an eighth of a mile in some eighteen seconds when without warning and in one seamless move we start to freewheel forward gathering momentum as we coast smoothly down 'Wooooooooooooooooooo!' (but surely the road is level all through?) and we're back where it began between the shrine and the signboards.

P.Singh is still idling in neutral. Man's clutching the steering and laughing so hard that beads of perspiration have popped up all over his brow. Disappointingly, we don't experience a rerun of whatever this was. I'd like to step out and try cracking it from terra firma – more like terra bloody enigma – but Man steps on it and we're out of zone and there's no turning around. 'And risk losing you to ether?' he chuckles in response to a minor harangue, 'You still have to navigate the rest of this drive.'

'Mark my word,' I laugh, 'this jaunt is going to alter me in some big huge dramatic way.'

'Should we be worried?'

'Not at all. In fact, I have a feeling it's already begun.'

'I'd better call home and let them know.'

'Our phones are still jammed, remember.'

'I'll call from Leh. By the way, where are we staying?'

'Don't know, don't care. See? I never used to be flippant about practical details. Too much practical can ... kill imagination.'

'I should know,' he smiles.

I should too, having spent the past year being frighteningly so, with precious little to show for it in the area of inspiration. Of one thing I'm now certain. Something will come of this journey – some grand epiphany – to slap me back to my senses. I open my notebook and make two columns. My list of Interesting People is reassuringly longer than my Predictable Bores. If this little black book were to ever fall into the right hands, the findings should be a cracker up their arses. The landscape has scarcely altered when I look up. We pass a milestone. LEH 35 km. One must occasionally, very occasionally, shift gears. 'Purely out of interest, how are we doing for fuel?'

'Not good.'

'Excellent. Let's not stop anywhere between here and Leh.'

At first, it had posed an impasse in the most literal sense, bringing military machinery engaged in building this road in the late 1970s to a grinding halt. The boulder sat in their direct line of approach between two hillocks; perhaps it had tumbled from one or the other at some forgotten period. It wouldn't have been at all difficult to bulldoze aside or blow apart, but for its accretion of prayer flags – indication enough that it was the focus of Buddhist veneration. On closer inspection, the *patthar* was found to bear the impression of a crouched human form: life size, smoothly contoured, and very much like the right hand side half of a two-part mould. A separate indentation a few inches away resembled the imprint of an outsized human foot. More astonishingly, associated lore pointed to an unexpected mystical root.

On his way back to the Punjab from a spiritual journey through Sikkim, Nepal and Tibet, Guru Nanak, the founding father of Sikhism, is believed to have stopped here in 1517 at the request of local Buddhists, expressly to help rid the region of a malevolent supernatural force. For days to follow, the Guru had sat in meditation at the foot of the hillocks, breaking only for prayers and discourse with local lamas. One morning, a boulder came hurtling down towards the meditating savant. On impact, the stone miraculously softened to the malleability of warm wax, harmlessly folding itself about the seated figure. Enraged at this turn of events, the dark force behind the act kicked the boulder, only to find the print of its right foot cast to the substance, already hardening back to stone. Recognizing its impotence in the face of more evolved energies, the Darkness relinquished its hold over the region. His mission complete, Guru Nanak resumed his journey to the Punjab.

In the light of this account, the intended path of the Kargil-Leh Highway was promptly realigned by about a dozen yards. Prayer flags have long been replaced by claret velvet, draped over almost all of the boulder's considerable height and girth. The floor surrounding the slight dip in which it sits is carpeted in maroon. There are brass railings along three sides. We have knelt before the impression of the crouched human form with our heads covered in our handkerchiefs in deference to tradition. A window in the velvet frames a very large footprint. The spacious white building that has grown around the boulder is the Gurdwara Pathar Sahib. With only the granthi reading softly from the Gurbani in the adjoining Diwan Hall, the temple is quiet. A younger Sikh spoons sweetened semolina into our palms as we emerge from the sanctum. Lining the walls of the outer halls is a phalanx of memorial plaques, dedicated by grandparents, parents, siblings, wives and children.

There are more soldiers commemorated across the road, their names inscribed to hundreds of steps in the hillock overlooking the Gurdwara. The top of the hillock is completely dotted with scores of little cairns, the tiered stones of their arrangement perfectly balanced to brave the gales sweeping the slopes. So many anonymous tributes. With a bit of practice, we contribute two more to the assemblage. At the edge of the summit, a small platform with an empty flagstaff affords a grasp of the surrounding silence. Directly below are the Gurdwara's dove-grey rooftops. By the dark ribbon of road, P.Singh is a patient glint of black and silver. I squint up at the sky and unblur my focus. The black and white forms, unmistakable in their exquisite span and incredible altitude, are two lammergeyers, sailing the blue.

11.40 a.m. Any further, and we would have sputtered to an unceremonious stop. But *excellent* timing. A power failure at the fuel station near Leh Airport ends even as the attendants, three of them, have taken turns at cheerfully cranking the pump. The counter whirrs with alacrity to the desired eighty-nine litres. The men comment on P.Singh's 'barra capacity' of ninety at the full, are crushingly less impressed by the distance we've travelled; they must see enough idiot long haulers, our numbers only growing each year. Tyre pressures checked, more julleys, and we are set to whirl into town.

First things first. The headquarters of Snow Leopard Conservancy (SLC), Ladakh Operations, occupies an upstairs room in Shangara House on the Tukcha Main Road. It is a merry clutter of filing cabinets and bookshelves, posters and slogan stickers, pinboards with maps and photographs of iconic creatures, printers and PCs with wild-scenic wallpapers, telephones and views of the garden below. Busy times: the desktops are dense with paperwork; a mobile buried somewhere is sporadically ringing a jolly tune; the rows and columns in a wall-planner are chock-a-block with names and figures. It feels odd to be conducting a conversation with a young woman who has crawled under a table to fiddle with some wires. 'So much to do,' she mutters in exasperation, 'and internet is down again.' She emerges backwards, straightens up to her full height (which isn't very much) and informs us that the man we're here to meet has just stepped out; something about Inner Line Permits for someone he's expecting from Bangalore.

'That would probably be us?'

'Maybe,' she says, finding the mobile and putting through a call. Her Ladakhi is rapidfire sing-song. 'Very good. Jigmet said to bring you to the DM's office or else you'll waste time looking for it. Come, let's go.' Good karma. And the young woman looks like she can do with a break from tangled wires. We troop into P.Singh and head to the District Magistrate of Leh's headquarters.

My only exchange with Jigmet Dadul, SLC-India's Programme Manager, has been one phone call (courtesy their URL from a friend of a friend) a week before setting out for suggestions on where we might hole up, followed by an email with a tentative schedule. The voice across the subcontinent had had a smile (evident also in a photograph on the website). Evidently, a special permit was mandatory in order to visit outlying zones; Jigmet would be happy to help us with that. As for creature comforts, the homestays were just upping shutters for the Season; he'd pencil us in at a place that was quiet and comfortable. 'See you soon. Julley,' and over and out. Until now.

The District Magistrate's is a post-colonial block with smaller buildings ranged about, complete with a predictable flow of faceless humans clutching files and briefcases. A number of vehicles are parked by the side of the road. 'Wait here,' commands our escort and disappears.

The parapet of the road overlooks a vast open ground. A cricket match there seems to have attracted all of Leh. Amidst lusty cheers from around the pitch and the parapet-hangabouts, the red-team is scoring mighty runs. The chap at the stumps must be the local Tendulkar. He hits a whopper that sends the ball screaming over our heads to crash right through the windscreen of an SUV parked behind us. A great cry of jubilation erupts from the ground; the reaction in the immediate vicinity is altogether bizarre. In any other setting, the incident would have flamed a minor riot. It has to be the air in these parts. The driver of the injured vehicle calmly fishes out the ball and lobs it back to the players and, to much backslapping commiseration from his chums, brushes glass off his sleeves and continues to enjoy the cricketing action.

'Better find a different spot,' says Man with a frown and takes P.Singh to the parking lot of a neighbouring cinema. The posters there are for *Khorwa*, an AIDS docu-drama. Our friend shortly reappears with Jigmet in tow.

He is an animated character, a little older than his online photograph but with the same puckish smile and a mop of unruly curls. 'Welcome to Leh. I came by to collect a form for your permit; it's good that you are here. Let's go in and get this done.'

The Permits Office is queued with men with folders, bulging papers and passports. Everyone seems to know everyone; there's a genial buzz of julleys and banter. 'Travel agents,' says Jigmet, 'Getting permits for their clients. This part won't take too long.'

The application for a *Grant of Inner Line Permit in favour of Indian Citizen* has spaces for names and addresses, and – pending approval by the Assistant District Magistrate – affords visitor-status into the Khaltsi, Nubra and Changthang regions. The Permit comes time-bound. The first of several clauses reminds the grantee to 'keep sufficient number of Photostat copies of the permit with them which may be required for depositing at each points of entry/exit.' There is no particular sequence in which a visit must be taken so long as one doesn't overstay one's welcome.

The week we've requested must perforce commence tomorrow. It suddenly seems woefully short. Before we can juggle some dates about, it's our turn at the counter. The clerks are efficient and courteous. The first collects a fee of Rs 10 'per tourist' towards a Red Cross Fund. A separate *Permit to Enter Wildlife Sanctuary / National Park*, more specifically the Nubra Valley and the great lakes, granted on behalf of the Department of Wildlife Protection, brings our grand total to 300 INR. The second clerk makes an entry in a ledger and swivels it around for a signature. The third goes bang-bang with a rubberstamp at our receipts and application. The Permit-proper, however, will be handed out after 4 p.m.

'Not to worry,' says Jigmet. He'll have it collected and photocopied and reach the whole lot to us later. His white Maruti Gypsy is parked nearby. The young woman drives it back to SLC, leaving Jigmet to introduce us to the Gangbas.

The homestead is blissfully removed from the bustle of downtown in an acreage of farmland on the Upper Tukcha Road. We leave P.Singh in the company of a blue Maruti Van just inside the gates of the compound. A narrow path winds along a stretch of cultivation and down between two blocks of rooms. 'This is the one they've prepared for you,' says Jigmet, pushing open a door.

The room is simple and tastefully appointed. Two armchairs converse over a coffee table by a large picture window. The maroon curtains are drawn to admit the afternoon. The wall-to-wall carpet, reminiscent of astroturf, has a thick lining of newspapers for added insulation. Neatly folded on the beds are two sets of olive towels. The en suite bathroom is spotless and spacious and the water from the faucets, piping hot. It's all perfect; we couldn't have asked for more. The window frames a kitchen garden, flanking the path leading up to the main house.

It is classic Ladakhi: whitewashed, flat roofed and with glazed windows, its woodworked details painted toffee-brown, and all of it set on a high basement platform. The rooftop is splendidly prayerflagged in tiers. To the right of the house stands a copse of apricot and apple trees in bloom; to the left is a boulder-strewn gully and a fringe of poplar and willow. A solitary apricot tree in the middle of the path is, somewhat eccentrically, embellished with a defunct pushbutton telephone. In the kitchen garden alongside, an elderly Ladakhi lady raking the beds pauses to bid a hearty 'Julley!'. The backdrop, stunning, to all of this is a section of the snow-peaked Stok Range.

A magpie with proprietorial eyes and a wonky left wing has all along been observing our progress from the plinth of the house. The katangputit – what a delightful word – doesn't budge as we remove our shoes at the front door. The assortment parked here includes a child's pink Crocs. The door is answered by a slightly anxious-looking woman. Her expression changes in an instant to a smile of undiluted warmth.

Yangchan Dolma and her husband Stanzin Wangial Gangba have been expecting us, but our timing has clearly interrupted lunch. It's several hours since breakfast but neither Man nor I are especially hungry. And it seems politer to not jump to the invitation to join them at the table. Intended politeness turns faux pas. Thankfully, Jigmet is quick to relieve an awkward pause: If we don't plan to eat, well, he'll be delighted to help clear out the bowls. The mood at once lightens. Wangial offers to get some tea going. Refuse that, he laughs, and he'll have mum, out there with the rake, take charge. There's a comforting familiarity to all this badinage – almost as though we've been around for ages. We troop indoors.

The hallmark of a Ladakhi home is its glass-room – designed to draw in light and warmth from the east and south, and invariably presenting garden views. Large windows occupy two adjacent walls. The floor is parqueted; the ceiling is composed of poplar beams and willow lathes. A small chimney-hole looks down into the middle of the room; braziers emerge from storage at the first signs of winter. Furniture consists mainly of deep divans along the windows, with low, carved wooden tables, *chogtse*, before them for food, drink and flowers. One length of wall is invariably worked with an ornate, wooden shelving system known as a *langs*. There may be a television. Modest or large, a glass-room is where families gather to relax, converse, dine and host, and to appreciate the fruit of their labours outdoors. It is a living room – in every sense of the term.

The one we are welcomed into is a veritable architectural jewelbox, the light animating Klimt-like effects of gemstone hues from the panes in the windows and the carpet-weave divan-covers, the handpainted *chogtse* to hints from the langs of copper and brass, children's books in an armchair (the child itself, away at school), silk-brocade cushions, framed photographs, luminous lama, faded-rose pink *solja* tea in fine china cups with lapis willow-pattern. I'm high here on form, texture, aroma and colour and quite removed from the conversation buzzing around. I catch a snatch. Man's informed our hosts that we might drive up tomorrow to Khardung La and beyond.

Two pairs of pins are glad for this workout. It is a little past four. The thin air is nippy but pleasant. Man, in his bomber jacket, cuts a ludicrously dashing figure. I rib him; he tells me to shut up and speeds up. The trudge up to Market Road – past other farmland idylls, across a bridge over a stream of boulders, past WWF and the dry-fruits co-operative, the water-bottling charity, the still-hibernating cafés, hotels, travel agencies and souvenir shops – takes us under a quarter of an hour.

For downtown's main commercial hub, Market Road seems surprisingly hushed. The few establishments that are open are getting a dusting out, in preparation for the Season to really take off. Business is brisk only around a party of vegetable vendors. One of the ladies, reigning over her patch of pavement in a broad felt hat and purple goncha, bears a striking resemblance to Wangial's mother. It *is* her. She waves a turnip at us and turns to her companions. The other ladies, similarly attired in black, mauves and browns, smile and wave and call 'Julley' in chorus.

I must find a public telephone to let home know of our current whereabouts. Get Connected Internet Centre (Jigmet had suggested, earlier, that he meet us here with our Permit at 6 p.m.) is not hard to find. It's the largest of its kind on Market Road. Their phones, ironically, are temporarily down and the broadband connection, enervatingly slow.

Man's going tic-tac-toe over his Inbox. 'When it rains, it pours,' he mutters, referring to a bonanza of job offers.

'Anything interesting?'

'Nope. And nothing yet from the one I'm banking on.'

Not unusually, there's nothing in mine that merits urgent attention. I manage one email BCC'd to folks near and far before our connections die on us. It's pointless sitting around. On the note that we'll rendezvous here in about an hour, I step out.

At the carpet shop next door, a sloe-eyed individual is vigorously shaking out a small kilim. It certainly merits less cavalier treatment. Save me kind sire, cries the little woven wonder.

Desire is the root of all suffering, I remind myself. In any case, I've sworn not to indulge in a single material acquisition for the entire duration of this journey. Tough luck, I say to the kilim.

This higgledy-piggledy array of shops and restaurants has grown, unplanned and narrowly upwards, from older foundations along the road and around darkly shadowed souk-like courtyards. It's not hard to imagine this setting in centuries past – jostling with mules and pack-horses and camels, the air pungent with the tongues of traders from faraway places, acrid with opium, salt, sweat and wool. Why, in my mind's eye, do I see a man whose skin is all blue? A man with bloodshot eyes and feet that are talons, hunkered like a raptor on a mountain of yarn. Silk, of course. Indigo, of course. I'm jolted back to real time as a fury of generators on the steps of the shops signals the start of a long power-cut.

It is a hole in the wall, easy to miss if it weren't for the grotesques staring out of the window. These masks are the real thing, not faux antique collectibles, their features contorted as sightless, anthropomorphic grins and grimaces. Come inside, says a gnome, drawing aside a grubby curtain.

It is dark indoors. The shelves in the walls are stacked to the ceiling with bolts of cloth. I slowly work my way around this textile treasure trove, letting my eyes settle to the gloom. Everything here has been used and disposed; the feel and scent of wear and sadness is tightly woven into the faded colours. The gnome is proud of his collection; something tells me I must not be here. But the lure of the finds is a lot stronger. Braided harnesses, saddle-bags and saddle-cloths, old tent rugs and worn throws, frayed chubas, patched gonchas, hooded capes, voluminous breeches, stone-studded headgear, rolls of brocade that may be thangkas. Another curtain and another room. For this, the gnome produces a small fluorescent-tube torch. It reflects unpleasantly off some glass-fronted cupboards, catching the eyes, inside, of large sculptured forms.

There's more bric-a-brac in a glass-topped counter. The torch is cold white through the scratched glass. The ammonites and turquoise, coral and lapis shards here, jumbled with tarnished silver beads and tangled silk tassles, are malformed, pitted and covered in dust. The gnome places something dark on the counter. It resembles a desiccated inflorescence of some sort, its shrivelled protrusions tapering from a wider base ferruled in old silver. The object is light as an empty seedpod and has an odd veiny texture. I turn it over. The nails on the fingers are distinctly human. I let it fall. The silver ferrule snickers on the glass. I turn and leave the curtained hole.

Something similar has happened before though the circumstances are different.

The European monk is robed in Tibetan-maroon. His eyes are deep iris-blue and he's terribly sunburnt. We're wearing the same model of Zamberlans and his are well worn. We are in a bylane off the Market Road, both of us waiting for the same public telephone. It's my turn at it next; two women inside the single booth are taking turns at the single phone and taking forever. My other monk, also European, at a restaurant in Khajuraho had sported a robe in sunshine-mango-yellow.

'Trekker?' inquires the present monk.

'More of a walker.'

'Artist?'

'Writer.'

'Close enough. What genre?'

I bestow upon him the title, the Rev Oxblood. 'Real buildings, people and endangered creatures. Big mistake attempting a novel.' The last bit has unintentionally slipped out.

'Why is that?'

I frown. 'It's a long story.'

'It looks like we have a long wait.'

'Well, I've bumped off all my characters. Including the cat. I have nothing left to say.'

The monk looks contemplative. I contemplate giving him

my backup tube of sunblock but decide against it in case it's viewed as superficial or, worse, forward.

'No hope for any of them, then? Not even the kitty?'

'Especially not the kitty. It was symptomatic of a larger syndrome.'

'I'd be interested to learn how you killed him or her. Unless, of course, you'd rather not.'

'Gunshot, from a balcony. It was castrato but that wasn't why it had to go. The shot, you see, was meant for a different character. So that character gets eliminated differently.'

'Aha. The plot thickens.'

'To the consistency of sludge. Sludge doesn't flow.'

'Oh come now. Do you have a date for it?'

'For completion? Not at all. In fact, I don't believe I want to look at the damned thing again. Ever. And please don't say never say never. If there's one phrase I loathe, it's that and different strokes for different folks and having said that and at the end of the day.'

The Rev is benignly amused. 'That makes four. But yes. A book is a relationship, is it not? I can stay in it, or move on. What do you suppose you will do?'

'I haven't the faintest.'

'Always a good sign. The answer will present itself in due course. Stay sharp.'

There's a sudden flurry as the women at last tumble out of the booth. 'Oh good. Would you like to go ahead? I know I'll be a while.'

'That's alright. It's all yours.'

All is well at home. And home is relieved to hear we are well; our jammed mobiles have been cause for consternation. I'm rendered a colourful account of a wedding I was missed at and who said what and to whom and how. My monk is nowhere to be seen when I leave the booth.

Twenty minutes past six. Jigmet is treating us to dinner. The restaurant is in the top storey of a shopping cluster, overlooking Market Road and a similar interior diagonally across. But for us and two backpackers at a far table, the place is quiet and the service, prompt. Leaving mok moks and thupka to the carnivores, I settle (despite a withering look from the steward) for chapatis and a double serving of mushroom soup. The latter is austere in both visual appeal and on the taste buds. More interestingly, our Inner Line Permit is in hand, along with a dozen photocopies of it for imminent checkposts.

Jigmet has a suggestion. If we plan, tomorrow, to attempt Khardung La and onwards into the Nubra, he has friends in Hunder with whom we could roost for a day or two. He'd ask them, in the morning, to expect us. He inscribes their names and an address in my notebook.

Man has had a busy afternoon. Having waited out the power-cut and then dealt with his Inbox, he'd found a trekking outfitters and proceeded to treat himself to a splurge. Evidence of the last, crammed in his daypack, are many pairs of high-altitude thermal socks, a spiffy headlamp that is frankly cyclopean, and two sets of convertible cargos and dry-fit shirts à la those intrepid explorers on Animal Planet and Nat Geo. And all for a song, compared to what one would fork out for the same goodies back home. I make a mental note to visit these outfitters. Only for market research, of course.

'So, what did you do?'

Should I mention talking-carpets and mummified parts, throw in a chimeric blue man or two, the Rev Oxblood?

'Not much, really. Pottered around, looking at ... this and that.'

His eyes narrow. 'Right.'

It is well after seven when we leave the restaurant. Jigmet offers to drive us to Gangba but a leisurely walk seems more alluring. We part, promising to call when we return to Leh.

The evening has turned dark as soot. We keep to the middle of the winding road, with only our footfalls to keep us on course. Something is shuffling up the bridge over the stream of boulders. Both Maggie and the Cyclops come to life at once. Blinking balefully at us is a great white *dzo* with a rope through its nostrils.

11

I surface from a complicated dream to a steady purring from the neighbouring bed. *Furr-click-furr-click-furr* ... Our room is bathed in a curious phosphorescence. There's a sub-marine quality to the light; merpeople must feel this way when they open their eyes. I luxuriate in the fantasy for a bit. It is nineteen minutes past 4 a.m. I throw aside the quilt, wriggle out of my sleeping bag and pull on some socks. The lining under the carpet rustles ever so slightly like secret mice; the snoring at once stops. I step very gingerly to the picture window.

Gangba's garden is experiencing a steady drizzle – so fine it could be mist. The tarchoks over the main house are limp and motionless. The façade is fast asleep. A blurred movement to the side catches my eye. The emerging form becomes a bedraggled white pony. I half-shut my eyes and affix a horn to his forehead. My unicorn walks purposefully through Wangial's mother's newly raked vegetable patches and dissolves into the apricot and apple trees. Everything returns to being still as a painting. Shortly, the next character in the silence puts in an appearance.

The resident magpie with the jammy wing steps stiffly along the roof-ridge of the house. He pauses at the end of it, effects a clumsy sortie onto the adjacent block, walks along that roof-ridge, flaps down to the mirror-wet garden path, marches all the way up it and, surprise! hop-hop-hops up the steps leading to our room. I lose sight of him for a second; the next, he's on our window ledge. He gives the bad wing a good stretch and swivels his head up and around. Does he sense he's being watched? Can he see me? His feathers are wet-ink indigo. I resist the urge to step back and jab Man awake – I can tell him about this later – for any move now may send the other flying. Instead, I mouth a silent 'julley, katangputit' through the clear plate-glass that separates bird and me.

We remain like this for a very long time. I am oddly blank of thoughts, which is a relief. The rain starts to peter out. Lights come on in the main house. The magpie flies away. It must be half-five already: Yangchan emerges with two cups on a tray.

She's bundled up against the wet and the cold. I slip on my shoes and a jacket, soundlessly let myself out and startle her midway on the garden path.

'Ah, julley ... your tea. You did not sleep well?'

'Julley. Thank you. Very well, actually.' The cups are fine china with lids. They clink as the tray changes hands. 'I was up early and looking out at the garden.'

'Yes, it is beautiful. Today you will go to Khardung La, yes?'

'If the weather clears.'

'It will clear. Breakfast at 6.30?'

'Yes, please.'

'Julley.'

'Julley.'

The eastern light spilling into the glass-room is liquid as honey. A window is open. The breeze wings in a faint apricot fragrance. We are crosslegged side by side on one of the rug-covered divans. On the chogtse before us, the butter tea is pale brown-peach. It is mildly salty; definitely an acquired taste. I run a meditative inventory of the china and metalware in the langs: the thimble-like tea cups balanced in pyramidal stacks; beaten brass plates, burnished dull-gold by age; a pair of long-handled copper ladles seem more ceremonial than utilitarian. A brass ewer (for chang, I discover later) with a beaky spout would be nice to take back, if one can be found on Market Road. That, or a twin to the stolidly sensible brass kettle.

Man, meanwhile, has established an easy rapport with little Tsering Wangmo. It probably comes from being a parent himself. The child chortles at something he has said and dives back into her textbook. Behind the glass-panelled partition that defines the kitchen, Yangchan and Wangial are getting breakfast ready. While she shapes some dough into plump flat discs, Wangial whisks eggs. He's clearly ribbing her about something; there's a palpable intimacy to their muted laughs. They move to the cooking range. Yangchan turn the discs of dough with a pair of tongs over an open flame. Wangial flips omelettes with practiced ease. The kitchen door swings open. The glass-room fills with the aroma of domesticity and bread.

There is Lehberry preserve to accompany the pita-like *khambir*. The omelettes are light as crêpes. Cardamom tea replaces the butter tea. Conversation pertains almost exclusively to road conditions and climate. It is exactly half-seven when we rise to leave.

Yangchan, who has been darting in and out of the kitchen, re-emerges with a tall brushed-steel thermos. 'Kahwa tea,' she smiles, 'for you to enjoy at Khardung La.'

Leh is just starting its day. We pull up beside a mani shrine and run thrice around the great drum of the prayer wheel, turning it. Its bells softly chime their blessing. We dive back into P.Singh. Man is as excited as a schoolboy this morning. And why wouldn't he be: he's driving us to the Highest Motorable Pass in the World. What happens after is subject largely to the vagaries of the weather. For now, the thermometer on the dashboard reads 3°C. It is close to eight. We're already at the edge of town and commencing the ascent to 18,380 feet.

'Don't look but we just passed an abattoir.'

'What did I miss?'

'It was *horrible*.'

'Oo *nice*. How horrible?'

'Ghastly. A huge pack of dogs were snarling and jousting around a man throwing scraps to them from a filthy green plastic bucket. Good job the windows are up; the stench would have killed us instantly. There were wooden frames to a side with guts and innards and skins hanging like laundry and sheep's heads and congealed blood and muck everywhere.'

'And you saw all that in less than a second.'

'Yep. You know, it's a curse. I try so hard not to *look* at unsightly sights and see what happens. Which reminds me, what's that word for *dog*? Zip-something? Zorry?'

Man frowns, negotiating a gentle curve. Khardung La doesn't seem at all as treacherous as it is made out to be. Not yet, at least. We're gaining altitude at a steady pace, leaving Leh-valley behind in a smog-like haze.

'Zhankey.'

'That's right. Zhankey. Even those bloody zhankey were caked in dried blood and bits of dead meat. Awful. Have you noticed the zhankey in these parts have dreadlocks *and* yellow eyes? Yolk yellow to be precise. Fine in an egg but evil in –'

'Please shut up.'

'Zhankey.'

The heater is on in our insulated bubble; the temperature outside is diving, literally before our eyes, into the minuses. At first, the snowflakes are barely discernible, melting the instant they kiss the windscreen. Within minutes, it's hard to see beyond some twenty feet. The wipers come on. We are moving, almost floating, through an unremitting opacity of white. The luscious tar-road has gone completely white; the salt-and-pepper mountainside is turning all white; the verge of boulders defining 'road' and 'drop' has merged with an amorphous greyness that is 'sky'. P.Singh must be the first to be so cautiously venturing up this morning: there are no other tyre tracks in the white.

Neither Man nor I have uttered a word in a while. There's a detached, dream-like quality to this experience. Yet everywhere in the enveloping reality, there is other life. A pair of chukar partridge bustles off the cliffside. Fat auburn marmots are bundled between boulders. A blasé hare is in no hurry to make way. As abruptly as it had started, it stops snowing. We slowly round another bend. Like a phantasm in a fairy tale, a lone black dzo has appointed itself sentinel of a gorsy ridge.

It is sentinels of a different kind about three-quarters up the way. The military checkpoint of South Pullu consists of several low tin-roofed buildings, deep in snow along either side of the road. The road itself is runny with melt. A drop gate across it is open at an angle, with just enough room for us to pass underneath. Above it is a long string of prayer flags. A signboard to the side reads *Traffic Control Post – All To Report Here.* Another declares *First Aid Available Here.* There is also a shed, marked *Mandir*. We inch forward.

Outside what must be headquarters, a party of soldiers in balaclavas and layered camouflage is standing about with steaming mugs in gloved hands. All eyes simultaneously zero in on our front number plate. We are signalled to stop. Man rolls down his window. It admits a jolting breeze; the reception from the men is a combination of wide smiles, julleys and good mornings. Two of them approach, very brisk and businesslike.

We are indeed the first visitors of the day. The good news is that conditions higher up are fine this morning so we may proceed to the top of the pass, and thence into Nubra Valley. Turns out, however, that our Inner Line Permit must be presented not here but at the *police* checkpoint a short way behind. I trudge back there with one of the photocopies, leaving Man in conversation with the men. The cold air is bracing. Facing the road is a large orange signboard hand-lettered in black.

SUGGESTIONS FOR VISITORS AT KhardungLA TOP

1. Always have a cheerful attitude.
2. Contact nearest medical detachment on having headache, nausea, vomiting, chest pain, cough, redness and swelling of fingers. There is a medical detachment at Khardungla top.
3. Avoid using toilets on Khardungla top due to environmental reasons. Please use toilets at South Pullu.
4. Avoid running and moving too fast at Khardungla top. Please do not exert too much.
5. Avoid consumption of alcohol and smoking.
6. Do not stay for long durations at Khardungla top (ideal time is 30 min) since you have gathered approximately 7,000 ft in two hours time. Height of Leh is 11,300 ft while K Top is 18,380 ft.

THANK YOU

Compared with its military neighbours, the police checkpoint is a solitary, cheerless shack. My entry coincides with the scurried exit of an all-brown apparition with one of those peony-patterned tea flasks pressed close to its chest. The pink-washed antechamber is empty. 'Hello?' I attempt, 'Inner line permit.'

There's a hacking cough from the room ahead. I stick my head in.

The room is surprisingly bright, almost blindingly so. The air is clammy with a camphory pain-balmy smell. Seated on a camp cot with his head in his hands is a dishevelled individual in crumpled khakis – a far cry from our dashing Constable Ahmed over Zoji La.

'Permit,' I repeat, holding out the document. It's plain to see the man is suffering from something far worse than a headache. His eyes are bloodshot and runny. *'Tabyath teekh hai?'*

He ignores my solicitous enquiry, wordlessly reaching out for the paper. A spasm runs through his body. He extracts a ballpen from a breast pocket. The mere act of uncapping it is laboured. He scribbles something on the back of the sheet, repeatedly turning it over to consult the entries. His socks have enormous holes in them. Memory: funny thing. It leaps to a quite different setting, different uniformed men, a different sock with a hole. The man cuts in: 'Driving licence number?'

I rattle off my number.

'Kya aap driver hain?'

No; my friend is driving.

'Unka licence number.'

I don't know it. My friend is in his gaadi.

'Leke aaiye.'

Fetch my friend or the number?

'Sirf number chalega.'

Surely mine will chalega?

'Ji nahin.'

Must not get worked up and incur some horrible altitude sickness. I cheerfully trudge back. Man is sharing news and biscuits with his new buddies. When I return some minutes later, the man appends the requisite detail to his scribblings and, clutching the paper, doubles over in a fresh fit of coughing. I find myself reaching out to steady him. He roughly brushes away my hand.

'The policeman here is not well,' I mutter to a military man who is passing outside and add: '*Shayad bukhaar se mar raha hai.*'

Perhaps he doesn't quite catch my drift. 'Ah! Julley!' he waves and moves on.

We've been on the road for almost two hours. For the first time, the clouds shift to reveal a powder puff of sky. In the blink of an eye, we're once again consumed by another rank of grey. The road, in parts, is sphincter-clenchingly tight. A looming dark shape becomes a knobbly finger of rock, jutting up from the drop with graffiti and *Gateway of Nubra* stencilled in yellow. We must be nearing the top. I sneak a sidelong glance at Man.

He is alert to the slightest movement. Without for a moment taking his eyes off the road, he breaks into a grin followed by a wild whoop. In this weird half-light, it makes him look and sound positively mad. It occurs to me that he and I have certainly come a long way since our first hill walk, in the neighbourhood of home, up an innocuous blip we've named Library Rocks. A stiffer climb, some weeks later, to a different outcrop, Lizard Rock. How utterly exhilarating now to be traversing this historic route – in the tracks, quite literally, of legions of traders, chroniclers, troops and adventurers. I have a sudden vision: an antique caravan; shaggy pack-horses and double-humped camels, burdened with raw silk and rugs and salt-glazed urns full of china and tea. They pass another caravan loaded with salt, dyes and pashmina. A horse in the middle conveniently loses its footing. It plummets in silent slow motion, taking with it a string of comrades fore and aft. The camels walk on with sardonic smiles. The vision ends as we make space for an oncoming quartet of army jeeps. All at once, the clouds part and we are unexpectedly afforded a blinding sight.

The white-on-black peaks are wickedly scratched against the grey sky. There is no valley to speak of but undulating, measureless sweeps of driven white. Directly ahead is a clutch of grey and orange buildings, feet deep in snow, with flagstaffs, telecom towers and signboards plonked, ostensibly at random, everywhere. We stop. There's a shrine with a pyramidal red roof fronted by a trident and white Om sign. A large orange plaque proclaims our elevation. More overwhelming is the sheer volume of blue, white, red, green and yellow prayerflags – zillions of them – reaching in all directions as tangled, clustered, wind-shredded, new, motionless and lightly flapping diagonals across the porcelain summit. It is -4° and exactly 10 a.m. I feel a great surge of eloquence. But it is not to be. My mouth spits out a sharp expletive.

It isn't Man's fault that his mobile phone has chosen precisely this moment to break its long silence. It isn't even the caller's fault. It's the ringtone, so understated in all other settings, that does it. Having started, I'm not above overreacting. 'Shut that damnedfucking thing off,' I yelp.

Man's face has gone rigid. He raises a terse forefinger. Too late, I realize this is something important. I look away; two yellow-billed choughs are wheeling in the wind; it is a clipped exchange. Not bad at all, I think to myself: my friend has just turned down a plum position – just like that, no hesitation – from an altitude of 18,380 feet.

'Good,' he says, shutting the phone off. 'Now where's that tea?'

Khardung La's little military museum and souvenir shop aren't yet open for the morning. A small detachment of men is busy with routine maintenance around the site. The usual pleasantries, and we are left to ourselves. A big black zhankey (I mistake it for a pet bear) looks up blearily and curls back to sleep in the hollow it has melted around itself. P.Singh's mudguards are adorned with icicles. Although the sun is blazing full force, the wind chill is punishing. There is nothing to *do* in this astonishing place. It feels perfectly suited to releasing all preoccupations to the wind and stained glass-like tarchoks. I have just the one niggle that needs taking care of.

There is an old adage somewhere about eliminating clutter, in any form that it may assume, in order to admit light, lightness and hope. Now or never. Out go metaphoric reams of manuscript and miles of words – all expunged from my being in one fell swoop. It is so effortlessly, remorselessly achieved it makes me laugh out aloud. Ah! This incredible sense of liberation. For all its muddles and ups and downs, Reality is altogether more enlivening to chronicle; it wouldn't be too bad a thing to start anew.

Like a sign from above, a wild gale sets a furlong of prayer flags flapping in celebratory fashion. Write about *us*, about all of this, they sing in chorus. I owe it to them to do precisely that.

We spend a good half-hour on the highest point on the Highest Motorable Pass in the World, downing the thermos of kahwa in companionable silence. Heaven bless Yangchan Dolma. The infusion is a miracle of cinnamon, cardamom, saffron and honey.

12

Who would have thought two sides of the same mountain could be so different. There are no clouds over the northeast face of Khardung La; the mid-morning sun is hard on the windscreen. The gradient feels more acute so the descent is quick, if rendered doubly precarious by the rapidly melting verges of ice. Whole sections of road are no more than dirt tracks, the grit churning with black thaw to run as soupy torrents. The mangled skeleton of a truck in a deep gully is a darkly glistening cautionary tale. The snowline ends. The lower slopes are covered in a glimmer of visibly sliding and falling scree. There isn't a hint of vegetation. It's unlikely the region has seen rain in aeons.

At the police checkpoint of North Pullu, two constables on duty look more than a little put out by the interruption to their game of carrom. I'm prepared with licence numbers but paperwork for these khaki-clads seems perfunctory. Some scribblings, no questions, and this photocopy is weighted down with a glass of tea.

Who's winning? I ask.

No one, replies one of the men; we're just practising. Join us.

Long way to go, I reply.

The second takes careful aim. To Panamik?

To Hunder.

Where will you stay?

At a friend's friend's. (Hopefully, Jigmet has got through to them.)

There's a barely perceptible shift in tone and stance: what is the purpose of your going there?

Tourist. Have there been many tourists heading that way?

Just honeymoon tourists, the second sighs, neatly striking a counter into a pocket. Wah! Come sit. Have some tea.

It would be nice to stay and chat, keep these chaps entertained with news from over the range. Thank you, I reply, but my friend is waiting.

Friend? (frown) What friend?

That one there, I point.

They peer out, for the first time registering other presence in the vicinity. Arrey, call him in! Now we can have a proper match!

Another time maybe, I laugh and leave.

'What took *so* long?' says Man, looking up from the map he's been studying. Now he knows.

The road skirting the foot of Ladakh Range runs in a northwesterly direction, following the course of the Shayok river on our right. That is according to the map in my hands;

the actual river is yet to be seen. We are cruising alongside a zone of ravines. The world here has been violently ripped to expose a great gash – itself fissured into gaunt rock profiles, at once reminiscent of Ramses and his ilk. Could these forbidding badlands really be the fabled Valley of Plenty? Could it be that we have missed a turn? No. The road remains steadfastly broad and unbranched. A glint in the gash, and a curl of water vanishes as quickly as it had winked. A trick of the eye? Wishful thinking? In time the gash begins to yield, rolling back and away for a sweeping floodplain.

The pebbled riverbed is several miles wide – furrowed by twisting and intersecting ribbons of water to create a vast puzzle of sandbanks and bare islands. Rising parallely along the opposite bank is the Saser Mustagh spur of the Karakorams. Millennia of melt has scarred the mountain with root-like runnels, all the way down to the river's edge. There is no melt draining down at present so Saser Mustagh is the texture of stale pastry, with a dusting of sugar to the tips of its peaks. A passing cloud casts a shadow the colour of mould. It moves like a witch, in tandem with the river, and us on this side.

Where the Shayok meets the Nubra at a Y and continues on its northwesterly passage, the riverbed has bloomed an irregular swathe of moss green. We stop at a high vantage point and step outside. Binoculars emerge. The oasis reveals a settlement, complete with houses minute as grains of rice and squiggly pathways like trails by ants. The surrounding floodplain is scored with a needle-fine grid of drystone walls, presumably demarcating arable holdings. The man-made elements reassure notions of scale which the mountains, by virtue of their nakedness, have all along deceived. The Nubra Valley is dauntingly, overpoweringly, insanely immense.

The camels are humped together by a seabuckthorn thicket, about half a mile out on the riverbed.

Man is the first to spot them; I've been scowling for some time over the map. It is well after 1 p.m. and a short way past Deskit village where we could have stopped for some tea, had Someone not insisted we plough on tireless on water and biscuits. As usual, everything happens for the best. *Camelus bactrianus* may have moved into the thicket and we might have altogether missed them for the trees. Out there in full-sun, the animals appear to be gossiping – oblivious, it seems, to binocular scrutiny.

'Wonder if they're wild.'

'Of course they are.' Of course they are not. Clever me. The last thousand-or-so *wild* Bactrians are a Critically Endangered Species in the northwest-Chinese and Mongolian steppes. Our own highly localized party is a genetic legacy of the Silk Route centuries. The present set would be domestic or, at the very most, feral – if such exotics at all go feral. Either way, what the hell: 'Wild as hell. And like all camels, bad tempered *and* smelly.'

Man smells a rat and plays along gamely. 'Should we?'

'Of course we must.'

Famishment forgotten, cameras grabbed, and we're out of P.Singh in a trice.

We make short work of the riverbed, aiming for two human-height boulders that Nature has plonked a little apart from each other, but felicitously close to where the camels have settled. Stealth is everything. One moment we're upwind; the next, downwind. There's an idiotic frisson to freezing the instant the quarry take note of our presence (which, frankly, they have from the start), keeping low to the ground and closing in again. Man claims the boulder to the left. I mark territory on the other and hoick myself onto it. The camels erupt in unison to their feet. They don't look at all agitated, just mildly interested. Any closer and we might have overstepped their comfort range. Thankfully, none of them seems inclined to galumph up to investigate.

There are seven in all, the largest a wizened bull with a bright red tassle in one of his ears. The animals are leaner and taller than the archetypal image of the species. This lot calls to mind, somewhat anachronistically, a caravan of flower-power junkies after a binge; all that's missing is the guitar and beads. It is clearly their season to moult. Thick hanks of russet hair are peeling off their humps, shoulders and flanks to expose patches of sickly-mauve hide. One of them settles down again and with surprising agility kicks her heels high up in the air, rolling and twisting in the rubble like a coquette on a carpet teasing to be tickled. Her companions look away with disdain. After several minutes of pleasuring herself, the slattern rises and shrugs off a cloud of dust and matted hair. Two of the others commence a complex ritual of mutual nipping and grooming which intensifies into some serious necking. Shortly, at some sign from Alpha Male, the harem troops after him in single file into the thicket.

The seabuckthorn is in fact full of foraging camels. The entire herd must number over twenty individuals, adult and juvenile, near-perfectly camouflaged in the tall feathery stands and only some of them tassled with the red ear-tags. The sun is warm so we stay put on our elevated 'hides'. Gradually, the camels move out behind the thicket and become diminishing shapes on the barrenness.

'Brilliant experience observing wild Bactrians,' says Man as we walk back, with particular emphasis on the 'wild'.

A great cloud of sand must have tired of its journey and decided to collapse along this stretch of riverbed. That is my explanation for the dunes just before Hunder village. They cover several square miles to create this desertscape – surreal in the extreme, but oddly appropriate so soon after those double-humped beasties. A more plausible reason must lie in the bowl-like form of this section of the valley, the wind currents forever powdering and sifting the stuff of the riverbed and, unable to lift it elsewhere, arranging and rearranging it in situ as these rippled waves.

Our footprints to the high crest of one disappear in seconds under the wind. The line of the crest is the shape of a fin – the sand rising along it like a skein of silk, cascading over the edge and crimping fresh moiré effects on the leeward face. The dunes are shark-grey, the sky turquoise. The crest sinks where we stand, taking us into the trough in a smooth vertical descent. The sensation is strangely weightless. We look up to where we've stood so recently. The crevasse we've caused is being rapidly reassigned as a double-humped wave.

I have camels on the brain. If Shand could do it on a pachyderm across the northern plains, what's to stop Ram from coursing far steppes on an ungulate. I can already see the title: *Travels on my Bactrian.* I turn to share it but Man – obsessing with his camera for some time over these abstractions of curves and dips – has transposed himself up a dune and over its hip. So easy to get disoriented in a desert; I scramble after his fast-vanishing tracks and come face to face, as it were, with what can only be regarded as *A Sign*.

The Bactrians are sailing fluidly through the shifting sands. It isn't a mirage. In delightful contrast to the earlier, unkempt set, this duo fits the archetype to the hilt. They are high humped, luxuriantly hirsute, beautifully coiffed, perfectly proportioned, elegantly paced and draped with tasselled, kilim-weave saddlepacks. The wind charmingly teases their forelocks and beard hairs. Both have riders on their backs and each is led by a diminutive local in flapping gonchas – an antique woodcut come alive. 'Why is she wearing all that gold?' says Man, suddenly materialising by my side and referring to the incongruously bejewelled and multicoloured entity on the lead.

A pertinent question. But it can wait. These saddles look iffy. Higher between the humps and a cushioned backrest would surely work in the interest of ergonomics. I try an alternative title aloud for cadence. 'Saddlesore in the Gobi.'

'Who?'

'Just an idea. Tell you later.' Temperament, next. No better way to find out than a hands-on induction, no better opportunity than the present.

The little procession is almost upon us. I scamper to place myself in alignment with it. It strikes me, at that moment, that I have a personal, albeit very random connection with the

A dzo on Khardung La

Atop the World's Highest Motorable Pass

Bactrian camels, Nubra Valley

The dunes at Deskit

An irrigation channel in Hunder

Willow trees, Leh Valley

Poplars and lucerne, Leh

Seabuckthorn and Pang Gong Tso

Toad-headed agama, Pang Gong Tso

Brown-headed gulls, Pang Gong Tso

Ruddy sheldrake

Chang-pa ponies and pashminas

species: a Polaroid in an album of my beautiful eccentric grandmum, posing with Bactrians, c. 1974, at Woburn (or was it Longleat?). These two, like those beauties, have the same bemused curves to their upper lips, the same long-lashed flirty eyes, altogether adorable in every way. The same cannot be said for the gold-dripping rider and her companion. From their archetypal getup and despondent air, these would be the honeymooners mentioned by the carrom champ. The outing must be part of some package deal.

'Is your camel friendly?' I ask the new wife, reaching up to stroke a woolly cheek as one would an equine's. Everything at once goes simultaneously bad. The nasty brute nearly amputates my fingers with its big yellow teeth. Having missed, it champs noisily at the wind, thrusting forward its head again and again like a dragon with halitosis. The new wife emits a needlessly melodramatic shriek. The monster's handler tries to calm it. The new husband, behind, utters an *oye* and does something that causes his mount to shrug the poor sod off its back. He falls lumpenly to the sand; his beast takes off, dragging its handler by the lead. The new wife shrieks again, twice, hennaed hands to either side of her face, before unleashing a shrill of Gujarati upon her mate. Time to make myself scarce. I scurry up and over a dune to find Man rolling, literally, in the sand.

3.12 p.m. The pretty village of Hunder is introduced by low drystone walls and tall curtains of poplar. Over the walls, rectangles of farmland are carpeted in new buckwheat or barley.

The main road is broad with pathways, some of them cobbled, branching to the sides. Rows of gnarled willow have sprouted fresh switches of lime green. The ubiquitous pink roses are teeming with yellow butterflies. Overlooking their neat kitchen gardens, the homesteads are quiet but breathing with invisible life. The air carries a resinous whiff of woodfire and incense. There isn't a scrap of litter, no bits of paper or plastic, anywhere. Happily, this is no showpiece idyll tarted up for the benefit of tourists, but clearly a long established and thriving settlement.

The trailer of a jeep backing up onto the road is loaded with farm equipment. We pause for it and then move up alongside. The urbane Ladakhi gentleman at the wheel is sun-crinkled like the Marlboro Man. He leans out to read the address I've held over from my window. 'Ah, Tsering Dorjey. Proceed straight, turn right at the first mani, left at the second mani, right at the third mani. Straight, and the red roofed house on the left.' He pronounces it *maney*. The directions are clear enough but perhaps I look a bit simple. 'Follow me,' he grins, 'I'm going near the first mani.'

We are hopelessly lost after waving our julleys there. A slight error in the navigator's skills brings us, via three wrong turns, back to the mani. Marlboro Man (or anyone else for that matter) is nowhere to be seen. We roll aimlessly down a road we haven't already attempted. It has been a long day; I am not exactly up for more excitement. A rant now would be deeply satisfying. I almost embark on one but quell it.

Considering he has been at the wheel for close to six hours, Man, I find, has on an inscrutably serene smile. He's been rather abstracted since the dunes. I'm tempted to ask whether he'd like a Polo mint, if only to wind him up a bit. Just then, we come upon a fork with a mani. 'Julley, friends!' he yells.

The children in school-uniform reds on a grassy embankment make a sight of impossible picturesqueness. We must look and sound like crazies so they are eager to assist, flocking around P.Singh like scarlet minivets: who are you? Where have you come from? Where are you going? Tsering Dorjey's house? Red roof; right over there!

13

The moulded plastic mask is a vulpine face with pointy teeth and ears. The child sporting it is about two feet high and swaddled in a red jumpsuit with rainbow-striped socks. Its eyes are wetly bright and level with mine over the top of the grille gates onto which it has clambered. Its voice is disconcertingly rough. 'Zhankey,' it says, 'Grrr … rrr … rrr.'

In the yard behind, a makeshift shed is covered in vermilion parachute fabric held down with lengths of wood and blue nylon twine. Some carpenters there are busy sawing and planing. From their gold earloops and upturned moustaches, the men look like they belong to Rajasthan or UP. The sole Ladakhi among them saunters up with a smile.

Tsering Dorjey is willowy and in his late thirties. He laughingly plucks the masked child off the grille, at the same time pulling the gates open wide. We were expected, he says, and our timing was perfect; he had just returned home from the school at which he teaches.

The child in his arms wriggles to be set free. Liberated, it makes for my legs with a deliberate, thigh-thumping sumo gait. I sidestep it. It veers towards Man who happily submits to a hug from it. Foxy next turns its attentions briefly to our wheels, veers off towards a pile of willow twigs, selects one, hefts it up to the plinth of the house and, from there, flails it about like a samurai. How quickly they grow up, Dorjey muses. But come; you must both be ready for some tea.

The house is a weathered example of the vernacular, its glass-room watching over the front garden and the gates. Evidence of additions comes as a range of wooden columns and beams along one side. A couple of new rooms, says Dorjey, which must be serviceable before the Season commenced in earnest. They had decided this year to tap into Hunder's growing popularity on the trekkers' circuit. We were their first houseguests; Jigmet had mentioned we weren't fussy; we'd be quite comfortable with whatever existed.

A little girl, still in school uniform, has emerged from the house, followed by a handsome young woman in a pink salwaar kameez. Introductions are exchanged. Dorjey and Angmo's daughter takes hold of her sibling (it is a brother) and hauls him backwards inside. Shortly, a sharp yelp is countered by a plaintive wail. Angmo laughs and rolls her eyes. Our daypacks and sleeping bags can wait; we are ushered in.

The glass-room – it is to be our digs for tonight – is warm from having soaked in the morning. The afternoon is diffused by sheer curtains, stretched taut against the clear glazing. The floor is covered in a well-worn carpet, lined along three sides with divans and chogtses. A cabinet by the door is crammed with high school maths and general science texts and a motley collection of playthings. A mask beams the likeness of an extraterrestrial being. Angmo brings in a tray of tea and assorted biscuits. I help myself and ease a curtain aside.

Once construction debris has been cleared, this elevated view – the vegetable garden, the poplar fringe, the distant snowpeaks – will be supremely idyllic. It's easy to visualize the house in a few weeks, getting filled with boisterous guests. Foxy, for one, is bound to be a riot.

Spot on cue, the still-masked wonder crawls in pushing a truck piled with more toys. He reads my mind and navigates purposefully. Since the time I was bitten by a toddler under a table whilst tackling a particularly spiney fried fish (not to mention the ensuing dramatics), I've been justifiably wary of small human beings. I'm in no real danger here of another near-death experience. Still, I'm seized by an intense desire for some time by myself. We have just this one afternoon for a walkers' feel of the village. It's already past four. I discreetly slip out.

The traditional Ladakhi latrine is an object lesson in concept and design, perfectly evolved from its environment. It consists of a mudbrick room, roughly 3 x 5 feet and 6 feet in height, carried over a chamber, at ground level, of similar size. The doorway is accessed by brick or stone steps; sometimes, a ramp of earth suffices. The door may be wooden or a corrugated metal sheet. The floor is a wooden grid, compacted with a plaster of husk and river clay. A hole in the centre opens directly down into the chamber underneath. There is no plumbing or electricity. There is a small window. The roof is slightly sloped. Of the lower chamber, three sides are walled with the fourth (generally the one facing east) exposed to daylight and air. The exteriors may or may not be plastered and whitewashed.

The present example is set in a sunny spot away from the house. Its floor is layered with dry soil, loosely mixed with bits of hay. The shovel in a corner is self-explanatory. The air inside smells pleasantly earthy. Not surprisingly, there are no flies; they probably wouldn't survive this climate. I'm told the pileup down there is regularly removed and mixed with manure to compost the fields.

The donkey foal is only a few days old, fleecy as a lamb and sticking close to mum. They move to the shade of the mani and stand stock-still like Nativity figurines – too late for last year's, too early for 2009's. I stop. How magical when long-dormant episodes, quietly filigreeing life all along, reveal themselves through opportune mnemonics.

December 1949. Out for a spin with a friend in their new Austin A40, Grandpa (whom I never met) and Grandmum had come upon a jet-black baby donkey minus its mum. Convinced it was orphaned, Aunt S – a ravishing beauty, a glad fool for animals – had decided on the spot (in her words) 'to rescue the poor darling'. That my grandfather had aided abduction speaks volumes: Oscar (the Austin) was practically fresh out of the showroom. Not surprisingly, Grandmum had abetted the exercise. I loved this story. Petals had the run of Aunt S's house. He kicked and bucked and slept in a sofa, bit the family dogs and daughters, ate a not-too-welcome houseguest's passport. The romance survived twelve months. On devouring Very Important Papers pertaining to ownership of the house, Petals was presented at Christmas to a convent's *dhobi*.

Aunt S's handwriting was like none other I know – sophisticated in its economy of strokes and connectors. She once gifted me a book on grooming dogs, inimitably inscribing it to Tosca and Wolfie. The little Ladakhi donkey looks like it's just been shampooed and towelled. Its springy soft baby coat is platinum blonde.

It would be a misnomer to refer to these as gutters. The conduits for water are shallow and about a foot wide, trenched as borders to the cobbled pathways. The water gurgling over multicoloured pebbles is crystal clear and has the taste frozen out. It must originate from artesian wells; the flow in both conduits is swift and steady. The sides are overgrown with ferns and Chinese parsley. As the pathways curve, so do the adjacent stonewalls and fences. In places, the water passes through gaps in the walls to cut through the fields. The farmers in one invite me to climb over and join them.

Onwards from julleys, the vernacular is a circus of syllables and diphthongs and zeds and leys. My own marvellous Hindi evokes gentle amusement. There's an easy camaraderie to this mixed group. I am welcome, it is implied, to lend a hand. The mechanized tiller – I've always nursed a fascination for these – is more tricky to manoeuvre than its wiry elder makes it seem. The puttering red devil has controls like a motorbike's, tyres like a tractor's and highly spirited vertical tines. Dignity is at stake; I manage a passable furrow across the field, forking no one's toes in the process. The achievement is applauded. Julleys, and I'm over the far wall and into a neighbouring field.

The conduit here has branched into a grid of narrower channels. Much of the ground has sprung new rabbit-ears of spinach. Other patches have started carrots, onions, turnips and radish. Small sandbags have been employed to direct (and restrict) the water to select beds. We had a similar system in place at the old house to irrigate the kitchen garden. A second, more-complex grid had served a mango, sapodilla and guava, a pair each of coconut, custard apple and pomegranate, and – a novelty – twenty Robusta coffees, their jasmine-like inflorescence attractive to bees before turning to ruby berries. Brick-dams breached to take paper boats by surprise. Tile-bridges spanned and felled at whim. There was even a Map – antiqued with tea, singed at the edges and stamped with the proverbial X in red. A sprawling ficus, a towering eucalyptus, a dapper Pride of India and sundry tropicals and exotics filled the rest. We had a rectangle of lawn bordered by heady floribundas and hybrid teas. Jasmine and bougainvillea cascaded the enclosing walls and spiked fence. In the very heart of town, the garden was a paradise for birding.

I seem to have been led here by the conduits for some very good reason – catharsis, perhaps, from things past. Whoever had worked this earth had done so with the greatest reverence. It's just the way it is in these parts: as you sow, so shall you reap. A redstart flies low, trilling high semiquavers. So-la-ti-doh and I'm over the wall and onto the other side.

A set of smooth dark rocks has arranged itself in Zen manner along a verge of green. The path is shadowed by willow trees. Any chance of reverie is shattered by two little boys, all giggles and gibberish, who pelt out of nowhere and take possession of me. One of them has sores all over his face. The other's nose can do with a good wipe. For a change, I will myself to not protest; there's no telling what might happen. The children are excitable and unruly. Still captive, I'm lurched to a stop outside a picket gate. One of the brats starts to yell: '*Ama le! Ama le ... Tooriss!*'

It takes me a second to get it. Like a warning sign, Muskmelon of Alchi flashes in my head. I try to escape but my captors only tighten their grip: '*Ama le ... gyogspa!*'

The woman who appears bids an abstracted julley, then turns a level voice on the boys which effects my miraculous release. The horrors take off laughing like maniacs. The woman turns away. All is quiet again – only the water murmuring over the pebbles.

The path leads down to a pair of whitewashed chortens. The structures are adorned with mani-stones and the skulls of yaks. It is oddly still in this cul-de-sac. I turn and slowly retrace my steps.

There is room in this Buddhist setting for other faiths. The wizened Kashmiri gentleman is henna-bearded and hurrying up the path clutching a green megaphone. Who'd have thought those were still in vogue. Perhaps he is the local muezzin, on his way, perhaps, to a mosque somewhere. He breaks step to exchange that characteristic Kashmiri handclasp. 'Tsering Dorjey *ka mahmaan*?'

Word certainly gets around. Yes, I reply, a guest of Dorjey's.

It is the carpenters next, walking up past the forked-road mani. Force of habit: 'Julley.' It must sound affected to them; it already does to me. They reciprocate with namastes and stop for a chat. They are itinerant craftsmen from Bikaner. Work done for the day, they are out for a spot of R&R and will later return to their parachute-covered shed.

In the yard, a game of cricket is in progress. The masked marvel is batting with a willow stick. The visitor is bowling in exaggerated slow-pace. Foxy should be one to watch for. The child unerringly connects each time with the ping-pong ball rolled towards him. Angmo, Dorjey and the daughter are spectators from the plinth. It is probably well after five, still quite light and very pleasant. I watch, unnoticed, for a bit and carry on down the pathway.

My compass – trusted companion on countless other wanders – indicates we are on a northeasterly course. The route winds past acres of cultivation behind high fences, leading onwards to an edge of the village. The few dwellings here are blocky and nondescript. In a luxuriantly furred juniper, two golden orioles are least concerned by the proximity of a human. Beyond a stretch of low scrub, the landscape is an abstraction of greys – surely the riverbed of the Shayok – with a range that must be Saser Mushtag scoring the distance. A dot on the horizon is an approaching helicopter, chopping air miles through the gathering dusk. Below, a great cloud of sand has swirled up from the dunes.

We're bundled up in chairs on the plinth of the house. The sky is a cobweb of stars and planets. I prod it with Foxy's willow samurai. A star comes loose and drops in a quick silver arc. Another prod, another star. I don't believe we've ever had it this good. They are falling fast and furious out of the black-indigo quiet. I set aside the twig and sit back with a happy grunt. What happens next bolts me upright.

It is an electric blue glow – single, circular, wink, gone. 'Did you see it!'

'What?'

Something tells me that to name It would be to never, *ever* see one again. That settles it. This is one Sighting that must remain my secret. Just then, Dorjey comes out to ask us in.

The family room is a little larger than the glass-room. The kitchen is integral, with divans and chogtses angled to face it.

The television in a corner is softly beaming Animal Planet. Foxy has changed his face for the evening and is reclining against his sister like a languorous guest from outer space. The pair is lost to polar bears on the screen. Dorjey lays out four plates and glasses; the children, clearly, have already eaten. Angmo ladles the steaming fragrant rice onto a blue-and-white platter and the four of us settle down to dinner.

What our hosts have referred to as paalak paneer is nothing like the slime-green sludge served up at restaurants. Here, each leaf of spinach seems to have been individually glazed and lightly tossed with slim tomato wedges – cooked to perfection and holding their colour and shape. The cubes of cottage cheese, Angmo confesses with a laugh, are out of a can. There is also an elusive ingredient or ingredients – something between garlic and allspice – which lends a delightful, nutty, sesame-y lift.

A commercial for Pedigree (why is it *always* Golden Retrievers?) causes ET to leap up with an ecstatic 'Zhankey!' He moves to the middle of the room and performs a quick series of steps, rather like a wind-up toy, all the while holding the mask up from slipping. Just as abruptly, he dives back onto their divan and wraps his sister in a crushing embrace. It crosses my mind that there is perhaps something amiss with the child's face. I try brushing it away but the thought persists; the possibilities are endless. Conversation over the chogtses has moved from homegrown greens and seabuckthorn camels (if confirmation were at all needed, they are domestic) to military presence, schools and medical facilities. The polar bears, meanwhile, have vanished from screen. ET jumps to his rainbow feet again. Tomorrow we'll be gone, possibly before the children are awake.

Come here, I say. He obliges.

Up close, the jet eyes are mesmeric. I lean forward and quickly lift the mask off the child. The face of an angel smiles calmly at me.

The granite house on Museum Road is locked up and vacant. The camels have occupied the upstairs and are passing around a salver of dog biscuits. Coldplay are soundlessly blaring 'Warning Sign'. I must hide the animals and polish the Burmese teak staircase before it's too late. Grandmum has climbed to the top of a flowering tree which she had planted. The speech-bubble from her megaphone reads ***THEY ARE LANDING!!!*** in that very typeface. The flying saucer is transparent, with REDSTART in neon lights along its circumference. The phylum at the controls is travelling incognito in a tuxedo. Typical of any self-respecting dream, I am immobile. I've been mummified, steeped in the unguents of my own history. I snap out of it in a cold sweat. The glass-room is silent – not even a familiar purring from across the carpet. I unzip the sleeping bag. It is 5 a.m.

14

A different carpet is having the life thrashed out of it on the steps of the shop on Leh Market Road. Its sloe-eyed tormenter flashes a 1,000-watt smile and, a change from the wheedling insincere come-in-dear-friend-please-only-look-no-need-to-buy, throws a blasé 'More inside'. It works. I enter, reminding myself to not entirely succumb.

The interior is a raised hall, stage-like in feel and proportions. Droplights in the ceiling have made pools of amber on the parquet floor. I step up in my socks; more lights discreetly come on. The walls are lined with two levels of alcoves. The carpets are stacked there in rolls, the weaves typically more alluring in reverse, like spines of books. The collection is extensive. Another young man, meanwhile, has padded in from somewhere. A brief, muted exchange, and the duo get to work in silence.

It is a negligible hors d'oeuvre of small pile-carpets: Tibetan, pretty, the somewhat cavalier manner in which they are handled a clue to their cost. A sampling, next, of prayer mats in both wool and silk with geometric-stepped mihrabs as well as ogee arches. I'm clearly being gauged for interest and intent; my face is a mask. Another muttered exchange and this lot is rolled up and pushed to one side of the floor.

The next set are larger, intensely patterned, Kashmiri, and unrolled deftly mid-air to flaunt their silken glow. As Sloe Eyes casts down each minx, his companion falls to his knees and strokes its surface, first against the nape and then along it as one might a pet wildcat; there's something vaguely obscene about this display. Because he can read minds, he flips up an edge and runs a deliberate hard thumbnail down the underside to demonstrate how closely, finely, the piece is woven. Some reaction, any reaction, is expected; I proffer a noncommittal little shrug. Maybe a dozen more and we are done with this lot.

The first of the kilims is the one I had seen a few days ago. It gives me a hurt look. It's hard to tell with certainty where these nomadic beauties had begun their travels. Samarkand, Bukhara, Ashkhabad, Kabul, Herat, Beluch, Tashkent, Mashad. Sloe Eyes has just set down a stunner in madder-root tones of garnet and pomegranate. I feign scant interest.

The tent-rug, handknotted by some anonymous women outside some faraway yurt, is a concentration of geometric *göls* bordered by narrow black-on-red zigzags, more of the same medallions and rows of ziggurats in fine white outline. The medallions themselves frame rosettes in lichen, grey, vermilion and biscuit. Unifying the whole scheme are bands of burnt-turmeric filled with stylized scorpions of black-and-ruby. The threads of the warp emerge past the selvedges as long fringes of ivory. The sole 'imperfection', individual as a fingerprint, is a corner göl that has veered out of alignment. A clock somewhere chimes five. Perfect. I look up and ask if anyone is game for some kahwa. It is a welcome suggestion; Sloe Eyes dispatches his friend on the errand. I sit down on the beauty.

The weave is tight without being rigid, the motifs very slightly raised as if they were embroidered. I trace a labyrinth with my eyes through the zigzags; the scorpions become amphorae. In a different time zone, there would be pack animals waiting outside. I indulge the reverie for a bit.

Sloe Eyes, meanwhile, is unrolling more kilims, laying them out in ever widening concentrics. It's a perfunctory exercise; we both know a selection has been made. The other man returns with a thermos and three glasses. Subtlety isn't his strong point; he reacts excitedly to something Sloe Eyes has wordlessly communicated. We proceed to savour our kahwas to the last drop in silence. Because my head tells me to do so – and never mind what the heart has to say – I inform the men I will be back a couple of days later. Not unexpectedly, they don't seem at all put out and start to roll up the marvels. I thank them for their kindness and leave the shop. It's unlikely my magic carpet will vanish while we are away at Pang Gong.

15

Yangchan Dolma has once again packed us a thermos of kahwa and a stack of khambir, this time for the journey up Chang La and the lake beyond. A little outside Leh, the Tibetan settlement of Choglamsar is festive with new tarchoks and bunting over the road to welcome a visiting Rinpoche to the local school. The road itself is lined with Tibetans in colourful trad that echoes the colours flapping over their heads. Our timing coincides with that of the lama's convoy, so we catch a glimpse of a beaming bespectacled monk in the lead vehicle before they turn off the main road, followed by the multi-coloured flock.

Beyond Choglamsar, the countryside is a semi-barren flatland, dotted about with military installations. The drabness is relieved at long last by a narrow valley, guarded at its approach by dozens of whitewashed old chortens. The road curves through an avenue of willows. The sun-drenched hillside round the corner is barnacled with tiny houses, with the multi-tiered elegance of a gompa, Shey gompa, higher up.

At the base of the hillock, a large body of water is surrounded by a high chain-link fence. A signboard identifies the site as a Holy Fish Pond. Some people at the fence are throwing balls of tsampa into the water. The residents of the pond must be a blessed lot. With each offering splashed over from the devout, the surface of the water is churned up by a riot of silver.

A short way ahead, the water in broad channels in a hydroelectric power plant is the exact colour of verdigris on copper. The Indus feeding the plant flows muddy-green and swift behind the channels. At the next settlement further up the road, the highway branches into as a three-pronged fork. The prong to the right runs over a bridge towards the gompa of Hemis. The middle one is the route to the Rupshu Valley and Tso Moriri – pencilled-in by us for a few days later. The road to the left is the road to Pang Gong. A signboard carries the perplexing legend: *Don't be gama in the land of lama*. We present our Permit at the police-checkpost and are waved on towards Chang La.

Clear skies, today, unlike the other morning up Khardung La. But the sun beating down is a mixed blessing. For the clarity it lends to the mountain-road, it also reflects violently off the snow blanketing the shoulders; already, the verges have turned to rivulets of sludge. The road itself isn't the best of surfaces, worn to rubble for several kilometres. The top of the pass, at 17,590 feet, is colder than anything we have experienced until now. Despite the ferocity of the sun, the temperature outside is -6°C. When I touch my ears, they seem to be in danger of dropping off. For respite from the wind-chill, we duck into the military checkpost on the summit. It provides us with our first brush with AMS.

The woman on a camp-cot has been hooked to an oxygen mask. Her husband and children are nursing mugs of tea, provided by the gruff men in uniform. The attack had taken the family by surprise: the woman was fine when they arrived but had complained, within minutes of posing for photographs, of a dull ache in her temples which had turned, in seconds, to a blinding mangle. They were heading back to Leh the moment she recovered enough to make the journey down. Perhaps, the husband tells us, they'll give it another shot tomorrow; they were very keen to see Pang Gong.

Only if the doctor says so, warns the soldier at the oxygen cylinder. Tea for you two? Help yourselves; there's plenty in that canister.

'Thank you,' says Man. But we've come well armed.

We leave the summit soon after our kahwas. The melt down the other side is almost a river. A red-faced cyclist is struggling uphill in a Union Jack wind-shell and yellow helmet and goggles.

'Good show, old chap,' yells Man.

The cyclist scowls and flips Man the bird.

Where Chang La ends and the Changthang Valley commences, there are more signboards of the Border Roads Organisation. *Paradise lies in the shadow of swords. Grow with BRO, plant more trees. We love peace but are prepared for war.* What trees, I wonder.

A pool of melt in the bowl of the slopes has frozen solid into a perfect circle. The expanse of white is surrounded by a coarse fringe of grass. We've stopped for brunch – khambir with marmalade and khambir with marmite and the last of Mrs Gangba's kahwa. My footprints in the frost quickly cease to retain form under the glaring sun. *Bigfoot was here*, I scrawl with a flint-sharp stone, and watch the block letters become a cuneiform muddle.

'We have company,' says Man, raising a toast to a nearby hummock.

The crest of it is dotted about with pebbles. A dozen of these turn into marmots. The beasties are stocky fur bundles in russet summer coats. They soon tire of watching us and begin a round of boxing and tag which progresses into a vigorous communal bonk. The orgy ends when the shadow of a big bird glides over the ground. In the blink of an eye, the hummock becomes a hummock of pebbles. We slowly make our way up.

The top of the mound is punctured with burrows. Some distance away, the ground sloping down is littered with balls of hair and dry grass – evidence of recent summer cleaning of subterranean dwellings.

The scree between a steep gully calls for P.Singh to shift into four-wheel drive. While Man takes the slope, I walk alongside, out of the way of the churning dust and guck. The downhill is just as tricky to negotiate. A marsh round the corner is riddled with islands that are tussocks of grass. The place seems to be devoid of any life form, either in the water or on the islands. The marshland ends and it is back again between gullies of scree and bare rock. I find myself subconsciously looking for vistas vaguely recalled from the album of monochromes. Aside from the futility of the exercise, there is the significant detail that the lake may have been approached from any of a multitude of bridle paths and not necessarily the well-worn trail under us. It is with thoughts of the summer of 1957 that we crest an eminence and are brought up short by the scene below.

A great mass of land has come loose of its moorings, falling cleanly away between two parallel ranges so that the sky may turn upside down and fill the void with its hues.

16

Spangmik, on the southwest bank of Pang Gong, is the last outpost to which visitors are permitted. Beyond it lies a perennially prickly border district, open only to local herdsmen and the army, before the Line of Actual Control between India and Tibet.

Past its military checkpoint, the village is a handful of wind-battered dwellings, cowering in a shadow of the Pang Gong Range. Fragmented holdings of arable land and seabuckthorn – the latter, coming into red-orange berries – are enclosed by irregular drystone grids sloping down to the lake. There seems little inclination in the village for displays of art or symbols of faith; its dismal air is assuaged only by the stark magnificence of the setting. A woman scouring utensils at her doorstep is, for the moment, sole indication the place is at all inhabited. A mangy zhankey slinks out from behind a latrine. Its mealy-mouth threats are picked up, more forcefully, by its invisible comrades.

It is a crooked little house at the upper edge of the village with the shadow-land of mountain racing up behind it. The family consists of two women who could be siblings, some children and a man. They can, for a small fee, put us up for the night.

From the windows of our little room upstairs, the lake appears deceptively close by. A fierce wind whistles through gaps in the window frames. I concentrate on sealing the windows with red boxtape to pre-empt needles of cold piercing in tonight. The result is already gratifying: the wind crossly buffets the glazing and lopes off to look for a different entry. Man points to a mouse-size hole in the tin-sheet roof. There is a knock on the door just then. It is the man of the house to ask if we have eaten. He seems to notice something is different with the décor but cannot put his finger on it. Man and I exchange a wink and follow him downstairs.

Lunch consists of Cup-o-Noodles washed down with Assam from our larder. We leave two more cups, for dinnertime, and a packet of Knorr soup with our host. His wife has a baby strapped to her back and is alarmingly pregnant. The water for cooking, she says, is from a stream in the mountainside. Her spartan kitchen is green-walled and sooty. The other woman is knitting something green. Clicketty needles; mannish hands. The children sit about, staring vacantly.

My thoughts this afternoon are all over the place. I am torn between a walk down to the lake, a siesta and a date with my notebook. Man, outside, is dosing up on Vitamin D and reading Janet Rizvi. On my way upstairs round the back of the house, I notice, for the first time, an opening like a burrow near the steps. Its mouth is ringed with large smooth pebbles, with a scrap of sackcloth for a drop-flap. Curled like a foetus inside is a mud-brown old man in layers of black. Before I can say julley, he reaches up and pulls the drop-flap.

I emerge from my nap at three. The house is quiet. A brisk walk from the front door to the lake takes a good twenty minutes. The full impact of it hits me the moment I stop an inch from the water.

The surface is completely riffed by the wind. A crisp line of white, salt, defines the perimeter. The water, cold but not freezing, is shallow and transparent and seems not to harbour any living thing. A drop on the tongue is alkaline; if this were a litmus test, I'll turn blue in a jiff so I do not wade in and instead crunch a slow mile, maybe more, along the salt rim. The mountains on the opposite side are taut as painted canvas, stretched all the way into China.

Shortly, a small cove in the pebble beach presents a stagnation of green-orange grass and blue-green algae. The surrounding sludge is pockmarked by big and small cloven hooves. A lichen-rashed ridge, separating marsh from lake, yields a deft tilt to the panorama. Away on the beach, a seated figure is gazing fixedly ahead.

'Colours,' his father had said.

I start naming the blues in the lake.

A rush of shadows blurs the pebble beach.

The brownheaded gulls come dive-bombing.

Rising away from the beach, the ground is an abstraction of rocks, seabuckthorn and swatches of white, all climbing to a trim of snowpeaks. The plan is to hit a minute structure (it is either a lah tho or a chorten) in the lower slopes and from there to loop downhill towards the village. Man sets, and maintains, a steady pace; from stopping too often to look back at the lake, I soon lose him to the textures ahead. The Law of Erroneous Estimates causes the manmade feature in the mountainside to constantly recede. There's nothing for it but to plough on, keeping the goal in line of sight. It entails working my way over a broad stream of boulders, flowing down to the lake.

The large loose stones, tumbled smooth by aeons of melt, shift and rock underfoot hollowly. One ill-placed step and I can easily snare an ankle in the dark voids in between. The stream is fed by tributaries of sharp grey pebbles like stone age flints. The rest of the ground is overrun by low seabuckthorn and other scrub of indeterminate genus. I pause for breath. A few steps ahead, thick quilts of frost are eerily reflecting the late afternoon light. The boulders appear to be afloat upon them. I remain very still, committing each little detail to memory. Something darts over a melting patch and freezes itself onto mottled granite. I cannot believe my eyes. A lizard is the last thing you expect in these cold heights. I inch forward to it.

It is a toad-headed agama – typically blessed with the face of a cunning geriatric. It lets me run a finger down its spine and tungsten tail. This is historic: up here at some 14,000 feet, my avowed revulsion for lizards seems to have miraculously vanished. I look up from communing with the surprise. A slight movement in the distance is the blue of Man's jacket. He is too far away to be hailed back; I could instead take the little dragon to meet him. It senses mischief and takes off in a flash.

The chorten watches over a deserted gompa. Viewed from this height, the lake is a swathe of inky silk. The snowpeaks on the opposite side are streaked copper-pink. A smoke-black cloud billows and dissolves at eye-level. The light deftly changes, turning the lake bluish-milk; the mountains, in sequence, get thrown into shade like painted backdrops on a stage. We begin our descent in the direction of the village with the sound of water leading us to it.

Rilled swiftly from the melting heights, the stream is a tarnished-silver ribbon with burnt-gold tussocks along the embankments. This is mountain water at its purest: crisp and astringent, faintly metallic. We get back on our feet from drinking of it; our beards are icicled in an instant. The cold, coupled with gravity and momentum, fuels a brisk clip down the mountainside.

The neighbours are building a drystone wall to pen their yaks. The only materials are melt-tumbled pebbles, roughly the size of a child's head. The wall, typically, is of single-pebble thickness.

Each tier is perfectly balanced, with gaps for wind around the pebbles' points of contact. The process involves hands of all ages: picking, passing and mechanically placing, to the sound of stone hitting stone as each pebble is positioned. The pen achieves the desired height. From start to finish, the whole thing has taken under an hour to raise. Everyone stands back to admire the project. The wall looks like a Zen exercise.

The howling night wind, raging in circles, seems determined to blow the house down. Happily, our box-taped window frames have stayed inviolate; a tight ball of paper has plugged the hole in the ceiling. There is no moon out tonight; we are hunkered down in our sleeping bags, staring in silence at pitch-purple darkness. My thoughts go out to the burrow-man under his drop-flap. It takes me forever to fall asleep.

We jack-knife awake simultaneously.

It is a single scream, piercing through the floor like a poltergeist. The wind doesn't, in deference, cease its baying. The next cry turns into a frenzied keening – a series of hoarse moans, sub-human, rising as wails. A door bangs. Other voices; the drag of a metal bucket; water sloshing. A pack of dogs announce themselves nearby. I scramble to the windows. Lights moving downstairs throw quick shapes to the black outside. A brief silence, and the vocalisations begin afresh. The thing is in no hurry to emerge. I start counting the contractions, three, four, several more, when expectedly, unmistakably, a mewl of new life rips open the morning.

17

The first of June. Man is chuffed that the baby and he share a sign. I have no particular affinity for the Western zodiac, preferring the Chinese instead for its vigorously elemental Horses and Tigers and the like. By the same token, the sign of the Earth Ox governs this mite. If he turns out true to type, his reliability and steadfastness must bring him and his makers great fortune and joy. We leave them a gift of Knorr and Britannia and drive out into the quickening morning.

Pang Gong in this light is the mystical silver of mother-of-pearl with an elusive vein of pink-aquamarine. The mountains are the ashes-of-roses of unfired ceramic. The peaks are still asleep in their cloud blankets. We pause for it all to sock us squarely in the chest. It is onwards, then, on the road back to Leh.

We've stopped for a picnic of muesli-minus-milk followed by crackers-and-Marmite. The marshland habitat, seemingly lifeless when we passed it yesterday, is animated this morning.

The air over the stagnant pools is thick with flies. Close to the road, two ruddy shelducks, orange-red and well fed, are wading knee-deep between the grass-mound islands. They are east-European migrants; it is the start of breeding time.

The male, distinguished by the black collar, works his bill urgently through the water as though he were searching for something. Success at last. He fishes up a length of sodden reeds; not quite solitaires but a symbol nonetheless. He hops onto an island and holds aloft the gift.

His mate isn't impressed. A desultory look, and she goes back to feeding; the marsh must be a bonanza of crustaceans and insects. Her indifference drives the drake insane. Fully stoked, he drops the spurned offering and splashes closer to the tease. His voice is nasal and trumpeting.

Boris: *Whaeh!*

Natasha: (silence)

Boris: *Ow-ow-ow-ow-ow-ow-ow!*

Natasha: (silence)

Boris: *Or-r-r-r ... or-r-r-r-r! Whaeh!*

Natasha (laconic): *Go-a-wah*

We leave them to it and walk slowly ahead. Other action is unfolding on the marshland.

A surly Chang-pa herdswoman has chosen this stretch for her pashminas to graze. There must be over a hundred of the dinky longhaireds, cropping the grass with single-minded zeal. A quick black dog runs endless blurs around the scattered bleats. Also in attendance is a clique of ponies, some of them sporting red collars with brass bells. The woman moves abstractedly, occasionally uttering a cry which brings the dog momentarily to heel; a different command sends it pelting in circles again.

The idyll is shattered when two of the ponies decide to fight – ears back, rearing, bucking, biting, kicking, the whole shebang. The goats surge messily en masse to the other end of the marsh. The woman follows, throwing dark looks our way as if to blame us for the rumpus. The squabblers abruptly stop and the whole lot splash at a canter through the marsh. We aren't left entirely alone. Oblivious of the exodus, one little pashmina is engrossed in mowing the road's grassy verge.

It's a ridiculously pretty animal, the hairs down its back parted as if with a comb. Its horns are curled like handlebars. It would be so easy to grab and abduct. Tsering Wangmo will be delighted to have it for a pet. Abi can harvest its pashm each summer. Yangchan will spin the yarn and knit a sweater for Wangial. Thanks to me, everyone (already quite content, thank you) is deliriously happy. All I need now is a partner in crime.

Man has paused in the act of wiping his sunglasses. There's a strange glint in his eye which calls to mind a hungry big cat. The silly goat is inching closer to him. It looks up and gets the fright of its life, transposing itself almost on wings onto the marshland, only to find itself alone there. Plaintively bleating, it darts about the quiet grass islands; its comrades are well out of hearing range. Or so it seems.

The big black dog shoots out of nowhere, flecks of saliva flying from its chin. The goat expresses gratitude with a nasty headbutt at its friend. A yelp and a bleat, and the duo become a dot of black and a dot of white, bouncing across the marshed expanse.

Purchasing a kilim is an essential life skill, right up there with changing a flat, flipping an omelette, knotting a Windsor. Man has accompanied me for the experience to Leh Market Road.

Secretly, I'm a complete novice at this. Mr Wangnoo seems to know it.

'An excellent choice,' he says, stroking his beard.

I nod in a suitably urbane manner. Sloe Eyes and the other shop assistant are standing deferentially aside. My gorgeous flat-weave tent-rug is gazing up from the parquetry. We've been admiring it for several minutes. I'm wondering how best to broach the delicate matter of price – none of the carpets have tags attached – when Man, parked on a settee, fixes my quandary.

'Dude, can we get moving?'

Mr Wangnoo beams a lazy-cat smile. 'Your friend is impatient. Come, please. First, some tea.'

The minions pour three cups of kahwa and take one to Man with exaggerated servility. Mr Wangnoo leans forward to me: 'You are married?'

I'm not entirely sure what that has to do with anything. A non-commital smile is best under the circumstances.

'She must be very beautiful,' says Mr Wangnoo, eyeing me closely. 'A beautiful gift for a beautiful lady, yes?'

I smile. Non-commitally.

With an air that implies we are above discussing such mundanities as money, Mr Wangnoo punches some numbers into a calculator and passes it wordlessly to me.

I have only a notional idea of the cost of a kilim. For a change, I'm quick on the uptake and subtract a brazen four-digit figure from the five-digit display. Mr Wangnoo unflinchingly ups the numbers a bit. I again subtract and pass the calculator back. Two more times and we seem to have closed the deal. Mr Wangnoo lets a long moment elapse in which we sip our teas in congenial silence. He then rises and shakes my hand in that particular Kashmiri way.

'I would never sell to anyone else at that price,' he says. 'It will bring you great happiness.'

Of that I am certain. It already has.

It is our last evening in Leh. Jigmet can only meet for a quick cup of tea and get back to work at SLC; I know we'll stay in touch, perhaps meet again sometime. The plan for tomorrow is to head southeast to Tso Moriri for two days there before our Inner-line Permit runs dry. P.Singh is already topped up to capacity; once out of Leh, we won't be seeing a fuel-station for a while.

Back at Gangba, Yangchan is preparing a traditional dinner treat. Tsering Wangmo is curled like a kitten in the armchair, declaiming in a throttled singsong from a school-text. Wangial has produced a bottle of whisky. Also present is a loquacious young man, brimming with ideas for attracting more Indian tourists. Abi pops her head into the glass-room, says something to no one in particular and goes out again. In a gap in the monologue, I mention the local tipple.

Yangchan, who has stepped out of the kitchen for a moment, and Wangial and their friend stare at me blankly. Little Tsering laughs with delight and is shushed by Yangchan. I seem to have put my foot in it and try to extricate it. 'I mean, when in Leh, a glass of chang ...'

Man, pretending not to know me, is studying his glass.

'So yes. Chang,' I plough on and, because I cannot stop there, '*Tintin in Tibet*.'

The trio smile kindly. They must think I'm deranged. Or plain pissed.

'Actually, it is ch*u*ng as in hung,' says the young man finally. 'Not chang as in hang. And you cannot buy it in a bottle like beer or whisky. It's freshly brewed, usually for festivals, and doesn't keep. Next visit, for sure; I am sure you will come back. So. Now what is a teytey?'

Before I can hold forth on Hergé, Abi-ley reappears and arranges herself on a divan by our side. Dinner is ready. The name of this stew, literally 'water-bread', is a misnomer for a steaming, aromatic carnival of vegetables and pasta-like shells.

Yangchan Dolma's recipe for chu-tagie

Serves four generous helpings.

FOR THE TAGIE:

- Sift 3 level cups of wholewheat flour into a mixing bowl.
- Add 1 cup of water, room temperature, and knead to a dough.

- Dust tabletop with flour. Roll the dough to the thickness of a chapati and cut circles, of about 2½-inch diameter, with a cookie-cutter or the rim of a steel tumbler.
- Flip each disc over the left and right forefingers. Quickly fold and pinch to form a 'tube', and fold again, downwards, with forefingers in place, to make a peaked shell-shape that is open at both ends.
- You should get about 40 shells. Set aside and move on to prepare the spices and vegetables.

THE SPICES:

In a stone mortar, grind together 3 whole black cardamoms, 1 tbsp black peppercorns, 1 tsp coriander seeds, 1 tsp cumin and 1 tsp red chilli powder.

THE VEGETABLES:

- 1 medium onion, sliced
- 6 pods of garlic, minced
- 2 medium tomatoes, chopped
- 1 cup of peas
- 1 medium turnip, diced
- 2 medium potatoes, diced
- 3 medium carrots, diced
- 3–4 leaves of spinach (alternately, pak choi), shredded
- Small bunch of coriander, chopped, to garnish

METHOD:

- In a large casserole, heat 2 tbsp oil and add the powdered spice mix.

- When aromas are released, add onion and sauté until golden brown.
- Add garlic and sauté for a minute. Add tomatoes and cook until juices are released.
- Now add the prepared vegetables and stir-fry for a few minutes.
- Add 6 cups of water. Bring to a merry boil. Check salt.
- Throw in the shredded spinach or pak choi and cook for a further minute or two.
- Now carefully slip the tagie shells into the cooking vegetables and soup.
- Cover and continue to cook, low flame, for 5-6 minutes.
- Serve in individual bowls with a garnish of coriander.

A wintertime variation features cubes of mutton cooked with tagie, potatoes, garlic and onion. The flavours, then, must surely be broodier.

18

The shadowless plain is taut as a drum-skin. There is no road, just tyre-tracks snaking and overlapping to a far vanishing point; I've stopped trying to quantify these distances. The air over the ground quivers. We stop and squint into the haze. Something, a wounded animal perhaps, is advancing through the silence.

The man's goncha is stained and ragged. His face is a dust mask, streaked with sweat like bloody gashes. Two flat ovals of wood are strapped to his hands. His feet are bound in bandages, with rawhide pads to protect his elbows, knees and shins. The bizarre getup, coupled with his actions, suggests the man is a pilgrim. The path chosen by him is formidable in the extreme.

He takes three steps and joins his palms above his head. He lowers them to his forehead, chin and chest, drops to his knees and stretches flat on the ground with arms extended straight ahead. After a moment, he gets back to his feet, hobbles three steps and repeats the sequence.

In this manner, the man will cover the entire length of his pilgrimage – literally marking every inch of the way with the prostrations of his body. Depending on where he began and where he might end, his meditation-in-motion can go on for weeks.

The pilgrim's eyes are closed. To the cold white dust blowing up into his face. Closed, to two strangers observing his progress. He passes, metres away, as though he were in a trance. He is not alone. Walking a short way behind, an old woman leads a donkey loaded with bundles and a half-full jerrycan. Three figures: each accumulating karmic merit.

Karmic merit. This morning as we bade goodbye, Yangchan and Wangial had solemnly draped Man and me with a kata each. They have packed us a batch of khambir for the journey to Tso Moriri. The scarf feels strangely comforting. The aroma of the bread has filled P.Singh.

Weeks ago, before Man and I set out, an acquaintance had a curious opinion. 'There's nothing there,' he'd said, 'Just emptiness.'

If I ever chronicle this journey, a significant part of my narrative will be about emptiness and the things I found in it.

Shortly after the long line of mud chortens, the purple rubble mountains and the green rubble mountains, we enter a saucer-shaped valley ringed by white peaks. The ground dips easily down towards a small lake. The surrounding land is dotted with rocks in oddly humanoid shapes. The lake is not marked in the maps; or perhaps it is, who cares; it could well be a seasonal catchment of melt.

The mid-morning sky has the suffocating density of cast concrete. The lake under it seems to expand and contract, crawl and recede. If I permit it, this landscape will gladly mess with my head; perhaps it already has.

Man's been rummaging in Rebdox. Redbox. I hear the jars of Marmite and marmalade softly clink, the rustle of wrappers, a lid open and shut with a snap. The parcel of khambir is warmly impersonal in my cold hands.

As I uncrinkle the foil wrap, I am engulfed by an inexplicable wave of unease – a prickling sensation of impending doom unlike anything I have ever felt. It takes a huge effort to surface for air; I cough hard and try to speak but my tongue doesn't feel right. My voice is an echo inside my head. The words don't match the thoughts don't match the action of reaching for the jars I am babbling can't be ams. All I've done is ride like a pasha in P.Singh these energy fields something vile here fata morgana quicksand we mustn't drive closer lake hungry stone fossil humans look away bitter metallic taste fuck head swims no don't panic rehydrate quick something sweet –

'Mardlame,' I say. Man, inches away, appears not to have heard me. I attempt a different word but this too emerges wonky. Martime. I cannot, must not, let this happen. The quick brown fox, I say to myself, jumps over the lazy dog. Good. Aloud now: 'The quick drown box jumps over the lazy fog.' Fantastic. I'm laughing uncontrollably; P.Singh is cold comfort against my forehead.

A faint vibration underfoot intensifies to an unmistakable

pounding. I glance sideways – along P.Singh's roof, past Man's shoulder, at the ridge beyond.

The Chang-pa herdsmen gallop past laughing and shouting their wild-haired heads off. Grit flies in all directions from under their ponies. A pebble goes ping! against P.Singh. The sound hangs like a prism before fading very slowly to complete silence.

We smell the encampment before we see it. The air is thick with green bottle flies the size of pigs. One of them blows in before we can up our windows. I corner it against the windscreen with a piece of tissue and crush it with a satisfying wet jizz.

'Murderer,' says Man, lowering his window an inch so I may flick out the thing. We crest a slight hummock and there, by the road, is the source of the pong and the flies.

The circular drystone corrals are arranged in a wide circle like some pagan installation. It appears to be a long-established set, no doubt reclaimed by the same groups of Chang-pa when they descend with their herds each summer from higher grazing. The corrals are empty at present but bear ample evidence, olfactory and visual, of being recently occupied; the animals must be at pasture during the day. Some ragged tents nearby are fronted by slim poles, flying, somewhat ominously, the tail-tufts of yaks. Wisps of smoke rise like plumes from invisible hearths; a line-up of solar-cell lanterns is soaking up the late morning. That it is all so quiet cannot be unusual: while their menfolk are out with their goats, dogs and ponies, the women have children to rear and households to keep. One of them outside a tent is absorbed in agitating a sheepskin churn. We couldn't have found a more opportune setting for declaiming from Janet Rizvi's *Ladakh*:

'The sole permanent inhabitants of the desolate region known as Rupshu between Bara-lacha and Tag-lang Passes are a few thousand Chang-pa, nomadic herdspeople living in yak-hair tents. All over Chang-thang, Tibet's vast northern plateau land of which Rupshu is the southeastern extremity, similar communities make the only possible economic use of this unpromising landscape by raising flocks of sheep, goats and yak on widely scattered pastures where the grass, though scanty, is reportedly highly nutritious. The Chang-pa goats are the source of pashm, better known as "cashmere", the raw material of the Kashmir shawl industry and now in demand world-wide as one of the softest, warmest and most delicate woollen fibres.'

I hand the book to my friend and reach for a Polo mint. Man clears his throat and continues in a silly accent. 'Although the Chang-pa are known as a good-humoured and cheerful people, their lifestyle is one which most of us might consider to be of the most appalling discomfort, especially in winter; even during the brief summer when the tourists [like us] are passing, their encampments seem to be on the rough and ready side. It takes an effort of imagination to visualize the transformation of the rough, greasy, matted mass of fibres, as the pashm is combed from the goat's back, into exquisite knitwear fetching enormous prices in Harrods or Bloomingdale's.'

The woman has untied the neck of the churn and emptied its contents into a battered bucket. Squeezing the skin for the very last drop, she turns it inside out and casts it to dry on the side of her tent. She then places a rag over a different utensil and into it pours the buttermilk. Gathering up the makeshift strainer, she starts to wring it. Her actions are deft. Her hard expression alters, just for an instant, when she opens the rag. The butter she eases out is a teacup-size pat.

The lake appears as though it were lit from beneath. The approach is level so we've come upon it without fanfare – no elevated foretaste but instead this sheet of luminescence, surrounded by marshy flats of acid-green. The beach is enclosed, as far as the eye can see, by a high chain-link fence with signboards along it. Tso Moriri is a protected wetland – prime habitat for migrant black-necked cranes. The fence is meant to keep galumphing tourists and Chang-pa animals clear of the nesting sites.

The minute village of Karzog has a minute monastery, watching over a clutch of minute dwellings. We've pencilled-in two days and nights here for a complete unwind before the last leg of the drive. Some of the houses have turned guesthouses with names such as Lakeview and Crane. The rooms are uniformly spartan, their windows peering down into the lanes or snatching glimpses over the rooflines of the lake. We've almost settled for one when Man spies a line of tents in the distance, with a curve of shoreline directly behind them. It doesn't take long to change our minds.

The campsite occupies a stretch of prime real estate just outside the chain-link fence. The sole permanent structures are a tiny kitchen and a block of toilets. Two men in army-issue fatigues are checking the lashings of the white canvas tents.

Choose any one you like, says one of the men; 600 for the night.

We have the whole place to ourselves. The last tent at the far end by the fence must be the best of the set. Like all the others, its inside is lined with brick-orange fabric and furnished with twin beds piled high with quilts. We plonk down in two chairs outside like mute sentinels of the drop-flap entrance. Tso Moriri, ahead, is still as frozen ice. The man who'd spoken earlier appears with two cups and a thermos of tea.

We quiz him about the black-necked cranes.

Not yet, he replies. It will be some weeks before they start to arrive. And then, only along the other side, far away, as you can see.

The other side, wherever it is, consists of amber mountains in a slate grey sky. I stomp about to wake up my feet. The water in a channel by the fence almost freezes away my fingertips.

Late afternoon, walkabout time. A pack of child-monks has descended outside the campsite for a version of rugby with a football that has seen better days. It must be their hour for letting off steam from the rigours of theology. The figures race and trip and pummel and snatch in a blur of bare arms and legs and maroon singlets and wraps. More child-monks, meanwhile, are scrambling up and down the escarpment below the monastery in a game that involves much laughter and clapping. Still others are silhouetted like bald birds in the ramparts of the monastery. The football suddenly breaks free and comes bounding our way. Man aims a kick. It sails up, up and away, sending the players pelting under the arc it prescribes in the direction of the fence. At some sign – seen or heard only by them – the children everywhere turn and get vacuumed up into the monastery. The silence left in their wake is deafening.

A gap in the fence is defended by a stile with a sharp drop onto the acid-green grass on the other side. The marshy flats, stretching away to the distant shoreline, are riddled with stagnant pools of algae from which have risen clouds of gnats. We pick our way towards the lake, keeping a small cuboid on the flats in line of sight.

The incomplete timber hut, open to the sky, has large window spaces along three sides. There's nothing to explain its presence. Perhaps someone's plans for a café got aborted by the guardians of the lake. Unmindful of our presence, a commotion of bar-headed geese alights just metres away and sets up a vigorous honking. On the water, several ruddy shelducks are trailing smooth slipstreams. Bobbing between the pebbles on the shoreline is a citrine wagtail. The geese torpedo down for a game of battleships. The shelducks put up a spirited protest but soon give in to the larger invasion and launch noisily away and onto the marsh flats. The wagtail, meanwhile, has been joined by its mate. There is a different flurry of small wings further up the shoreline. We approach slowly, stopping every few steps.

Another first: the horned larks in the pebbles are perfectly camouflaged. As the birds work the ground side by side, the male of the species can't seem to keep his eyebrow-tufts from twitching up and down every few seconds.

We've been tramping at a steady pace along the edge of the lake. Man's somewhere behind me; at least, I suppose he still is. I stop, at some point, to soak it all in – the sweep, the silence, this crystalline stillness.

A low whistle is a signal for me to turn back.

The sky is a wash of magenta and cyan with a solitary yellow star suspended in it. In the undulating blackness beneath, a barely perceptible cluster of lights – so faint they might vanish if I blink – is a measure of how far we have walked from the village.

The factotums of the campsite have invited us to the kitchen while they get our dinner going. It's really the same old fare from our dry supplies, with some stir-fried veg to lend the noodles a lift. The more garrulous of the two men narrates his life story: dyed in the wool Zanskari, black sheep of the family, stint in the army (cook), the comparative ease of minding this place, that sort of thing. His companion, meanwhile, has readied their dinner of dal and chapatis. They want us to stay while they eat – starved for conversation – and bribe us with coffee.

I like this warm sooty shack and am quite happy to sit back and switch off. When we finally step out into a full moon night, the temperature has dipped enough to freeze the channel in front of our tent.

19

'Going for a walk,' announces Man. This is one of those mornings when all conversation has been reduced to gruff statements of intent.

We have driven up after breakfast to a slight eminence of land outside the village. The ground in front slopes steeply to the lake and up behind us into a pleat of hills. From my spot by a lone cairn, the scene resembles a topography-model in a museum vitrine. If I crane my neck and look down to the left, an edge of Karzog is visible in the distance; unless someone is armed with a telescope, it's unlikely we can be seen from there.

P.Singh is parked nearby. Man collects a bottle of water and his camera, sticks on his hat and almost immediately settles into his steady even pace on the uneven terrain. Without breaking step, he turns abruptly, retraces his steps and hands me the master key to P.Singh. Odd chap, my pal.

'Later.'

'Later,' I reply.

The beauty of these mountains is that one can see forever across their surfaces without a thing to obscure the line of sight. Man's making a beeline for the closest hill. Closest, being half a mile away; hill, being a wee mountain. But of course he's going to climb it. Which means I'm going to be here for a very long time.

As I watch with interest, the vivid blue of Man's jacket is soon rendered anonymous by the pointillist landscape. Before I lose him completely to it, I unlock P.Singh for the binoculars and quickly retrieve a speck of movement where the ground is about to become the hill. I then fish out my notebook, a bottle of water and my Turkomani nomad.

Back at my spot by the cairn, I spread out the kilim. Heavens, what a find; the colours come completely awake under the sky. Another quick check on Man – he has begun a lithe zigzag up the gradient – and I lie flat on my front and open the notebook in the shadow of my head. Nothing deep and profound to report today, no telling insights into my rich inner life, so it's really an annotated checklist of good-karma katas, the prostration-pilgrim, spook-lake, Chang-pa lady, fence, signboards, child-monks, bird-sightings, living arrangements, manly silences and the fact that I haven't slept a wink through the second half of last night thanks to the honking of a zillion geese and a banshee wind hell-bent on entering our tent. A wonder I am still lucid. I close the entry with *M hillwalking; indulgence inaugurated Tso Moriri.*

The sun is heavy on my back. I wriggle out of my jacket and roll it into an elbow-rest, resist a sudden urge to strip and dose up on Vit D. When I peer through the binoculars again, M is nowhere to be found.

I pan a slow zigzag of the section where I'd last seen him. Odd. He couldn't possibly have flapped up and over the other side in the ten-or-so minutes that I've been scribbling. As I inch up and down the hillside, there's a twitch of movement in the boulders there.

The quick red fox has nipped out from behind a boulder and stands quiveringly still. That the delight is at all there is betrayed by the breeze in its tail. Something, a lizard or rodent, has caught its eye. It crouches for a moment before springing into the air and landing a few feet away.

Foxy seems to have missed his quarry. From the deep rust of his pelt, he has to be a he. He gives himself a good shake and darts now as a short streak uphill. When he crouches there, he almost becomes one with the scree. His pointy head is in profile; his ears are flat by the side of his head and the rest of him has gone rigid. I follow the diagonal of his line of sight. There's no mistaking the hat on a boulder several yards away. After what feels like an eternity – there's a crick in my neck and my eyes are smarting – the fox starts to crawl on all fours towards the boulder wearing the hat. When he is barely a foot away, he springs up and takes off in a flash.

The hat gets to its feet, bringing the rest of Man into sight. He must be utterly euphoric. After a moment, he turns and waves and resumes his trudge uphill. I push myself up and roll onto my back. The sun is blinding; I shut my eyes to a white darkness. It isn't the greatest position for a nap so I roll forward and on my front again and make a cushion of the jacket.

The breeze has flicked up a corner of the kilim. I brush away some grit and comb my fingers through the fringe. I am quite weightless as we lift and skim up the gradient, gently at first and building up speed as we sail over foxes and boulders and wolves in sheep-pelt, dipping and rising and cresting the hill to hover above the figure in the skyline, just for a moment to smile and wave and dive over into the other side, a green valley dotted with tiny houses, and rising further away in the horizon . . . as Hokusai's Wave where they glide past its concave dodging icicles like spearheads into a dark cave of stalagmites and stalactites which one is which bursting into open sky alongside geese on the wing over crystal water glinting colours of prayer flags up the shoreline an army of menhirs become monks riding cranes please fasten your seatbelt but there is no seatbelt hang on to the fringe smooth landing grit blowing poison darts into my face.

I wake up then. Man is sitting by the cairn, demolishing a packet of cookies.

'Did you just get back?'

'Yep.'

'How long have you been away?'

He ponders the question for a moment. 'Maybe an hour and a half to the top. An hour and a half up there. The descent was quicker.'

I sit up and stare out at the lake.

20

It was bound to happen sooner or later. Like it or not, this is it. Our last day in Ladakh. If we stick to the plot and don't get sidetracked, we should be in the Spiti Valley of Himachal Pradesh before tonight. Man's got it into his head to reorganize the boot of P.Singh. I can think of better ways of delaying our exit.

The lake is obscured in a thick wad of mist. The marsh flats are quiet in the ghost-green light. No shelducks or geese and certainly no black-necked cranes. Next time, I tell Tso Moriri; don't go changing meanwhile.

When I get back to camp, I'm told Man has taken a 'box' up to the gompa.

Very intriguing. P.Singh is locked. I run a quick inventory through the rear windscreen. Redbox, tick. Backpacks, tick. Tripod, tick. Box full of P.Singh thingybobs, tick. Emergency jerrycan, tick. Carton of remaindered soup-packets and cups-o-ramen, missing. I make no mention of said item when Man returns from the gompa with an extra spring in his step. Another round of teas and we pull out of the campsite at 8 a.m.

The drive northwest out of Karzog to connect with the Leh–Manali Highway promises another lake along the way. Progress is slow over grit and more grit, and not a thing to evoke comment. The silence which had set the mood of the drive has hardened into a wall of ice. I wonder, idly, what it will take to melt it. Our windows are up to keep out the wind. I try to recap the events of yesterday and fail miserably. I uncrease my frown and focus on the tracks reeling us into the ever-receding distance.

Tso Kar is a puddle compared to Pang Gong and Tso Moriri. The shoreline is encrusted in crystalline white sweated up by the lake, in turn encircled by a broad ring of marsh-slime. We've stopped midway along the lakeside. A range on the opposite shoreline looks like it were cast from a mould in its symmetry of peaks, each scalloped with an identical valley in which the snow has drifted and settled like a stencilled motif. All of this is mirrored in the lake. For something so natural, it's an oddly unnatural effect. Man taps our wall of silence and points to his right.

The ground there is an easy gradient of red grit. In the middle distance are two forms – completely motionless and identical as twins. *Vulpes vulpes*, yesterday; *Equus kiang* today. Thoughts gallop back to 1989 and a setting not unlike this, even if there were no snow peaks or lake there but an endless heat-haze where cracked earth met hard sky. *Equus hemionus* on the Little Rann of Kutch were compact and all-white. Here, their taller relatives are packed into bodysuits of pale-jasper and white with chiselled manes tapering as a black stripe from nape to tail. The kiangs are alert to the slightest click. I shut my door as softly as I can; to step out now would be to send them flying.

A ghost-village awaits at the far edge of the lake. The gompa on a ridge too seems bereft of life; the prayer flags in its rooflines are blown to shreds. The track loops past a huddle of dwellings. The door of a house is swinging on its hinges. A jeep on collapsed tyres has been appropriated as the den of some hairy beast. Balls of grass roll aimlessly in the grit, settle for a moment and are blown about again. The wind chases us out of the village and onto more bare plains. A faint promise of greenery in the distance grows at our approach into a marshland.

The track hugs the side of the marshland. A small clearing presents a bubbling hot spring. The sulphurous smell is overpowering but not enough to mask the pong flying over from an encampment. An ironic redefinition of the whole nomadic lifestyle, each black yak-hair tent has a battered Maruti Gypsy jeep parked next to it. Yet these herdsmen also retain their ponies. Riding straight at us is a party of men, typically wild-haired and madly screaming. They veer off the track and trot up alongside.

They are an amicable set: Keep to the track, they reply, and you will shortly connect with the Manali–Leh Highway.

In hindsight, I realize I ought to have phrased my question a little differently.

A pancake-flat pasture lies stretched between a mountainous frill. We've been bumping along at less than twenty kmph. Out to the left, a long trail of smoke has risen from the grassland, inscribing a steady course parallel to our track.

'Look. A train.'

'There are no trains in Ladakh,' Man reminds me.

But the plume of smoke has made short work of the miles between us and it. There must be a curve in the tracks; it will soon cross ours to reach this side of the grassland. We stop as one would at a railway crossing. It is a train all right – not the metallic, clanging, choo-choo kind, but a single line of forty-three kiangs, foals and parents, burning up the cold mid-morning.

We are lost. We have an argument. We turn around on the Manali–Leh Highway so that it becomes the Leh–Manali Highway – a matter of perspective, ultimately – and for the next sixty minutes retrace our tracks in brittle silence. We find the fork in the road that I had missed. We proceed down it and enter the Moore Plains. We stop somewhere in the middle of this strangeness. The mood and the setting are perfect for an out-of-body experience so I shoot myself vertically up and out through the roof to join the lammergeyers in the sky.

P.Singh is an ant on a china plate which a master-confectioner has dusted with cocoa and wavy lines in lighter chocolate. Arranged in studied disorder along the rim are assorted sins. Chocolate-chip cookie and walnut-nugget cake, honey-currant twist and mocha-truffle muffin, caramel-cream toffee and ganache-florentine, nougat-something and praline-something-else – variously tipped, streaked, layered and slathered in whipped cream. I could remain afloat forever, gazing down lovingly. But look: trouble is brewing near nut-nugget hill. I free-fall into the ant and fasten my seatbelt.

Man ups the windows and steps on it but there's no way we're going to outsmart the dust devils. They've whirled up everywhere, closing in like flying-lamas on speed; perhaps that's what they are, guardians of the plains. One hits us squarely and dies on the windscreen, burying us in a chiaroscuro haze. The mood of the past hour lifts the moment a feather duster emerges from hiding.

The Gata Loops are a set of twenty-one switchbacks in a proper tarred road, swirled like fettuccine where Lachung La slides from 15,302 feet for a drink from a swift river of jade green. It goes without saying that negotiating the loops calls for precise co-ordination between eyes, feet and gears. That plenty of others before us have shortened the distance from the top to the bottom is borne out by tracks in the bare ground between one loop and the next – all the way to the lowermost switchback.

From where we have stopped for a breather, all the loops are clearly visible, and clear of any traffic going down or climbing uphill.

'Want to?'

'Of course.' The moment I say it, I feel horribly irresponsible. But too late.

'Here goes,' he says, nudging P.Singh off-road on a wing and a prayer down the 120° incline. It would be even more stupid to keep my eyes shut, so I will them resolutely open and keep count of the loops we are shooting. One. Two. Three. No rush, adrenalin or otherwise, or maybe I'm jaded. Four. Five. Onwards from six – why push our luck – we take the remaining switchbacks as they are meant to be taken.

We've stopped by the side of the river.

'That was a damned fool thing to do,' says Man thoughtfully. 'Let's not tell our mums.'

'Let's not,' I agree, reaching round for a bottle of water and something to eat. The last of our granola bars are missing. So is a half-full packet of cookies.

'Did you also empty out Redbox in your ... fit of generosity?' I hope very much, for his sake, that he's kept his hands off it.

'Don't know what you're on about.'

5.42 p.m. Baralacha La. The white SUV has swerved round the corner and comes hurtling without a care in the world that we are in the uphill. The chap at the wheel brakes a few metres away in the middle of the road and then makes no move whatever to shift back or aside, instead shutting off the ignition and sitting back in his seat.

The mountainside to Man's right is a great glacial wall of compacted white. All but scraping my side of P.Singh is a parapet of ice that the sun has sharply crenellated. A tricky blind spot prevents us – even if we were to consider it – from shifting into reverse. It is the start of a curious impasse.

Despite the late hour, the La is bathed in hostile hospital-blue sunlight. The fuckwit at the wheel has doughy features and a vermilion cast-mark smeared to his forehead. His counterpart in the other seat is decorated with a handlebar moushtache. A pimply boy wedged between them wears a ferocious face, possibly from having his balls routinely smashed by the gearshift. We could be stuck here forever. Man rolls down his window and urges them to reverse.

The fuckwit responds with a shooing motion of his hand. He then affects a posture of great comfort, leaning back with his hands behind his head. It is so ludicrous a sight I start to laugh. Not a good thing. The lump opens his door and thumps down to P.Singh. Man promptly slides up his window, leaving just enough space to say: 'Vehicles moving uphill have right of way, sir. Please reverse so that we can proceed.'

The response, in Hindi, is succinct: *Right-shight kuch nahin. Tum reverse karo.*

'But sir,' begins Man: 'Anyone who knows how to drive will tell you –'

We'll see who wins, smirks the lout and goes back to his SUV.

'Pearls before swine,' I sigh, unfastening my seatbelt and opening my door an inch. There is room between us and the ice-ridge for my lissom self to slip outside.

'Where do you think you're going?'

'I think I'll have a word with them.'

I haven't quite bargained for Man's rage. That's a surfeit of fucks in the same sentence.

'No need to get shirty with me, you know. I was just trying to be helpful.'

'Like hell. Did you get a good look at that sod? Don't put it past him to put a bullet through your numbskull.'

The sod's companion, meanwhile, has stepped out for a pee. The cabin light suddenly comes on in the SUV. The rear is crammed with women and children like big and small goldfish, all engaged in a feeding frenzy. One of the women passes a bag of Lays to the pimply boy. He rips it open and proceeds to gorge, now and then handing his immediate neighbours a chip. When the bag is empty, he flings it outside.

'Sick,' I mutter.

The word is a charm. A little girl leans forward and barfs over the boy. He swings round and registers a slap to her fish face, simultaneously wiping the goo off his jacket. The stench must serve as a trigger for a pukefest. A woman in the middle sticks her head out of the window for projectile vomiting which peters out as green and orange gobs down the front of the door. She falls back into her seat and then scrambles forth again, hurling the dregs of her stomach onto the lout at the wheel. Something they ate, or good old AMS: the rest of the sisterhood starts to violently heave. In the absence of choice, the road hog can only back up, letting us pass so they may race downhill.

6.50 p.m. The happy-people café at the base of Baralacha La is a circular parachute-skin tent like a grounded spaceship. The boulders surrounding the tent are painted with *om mani padme hums*, Woodstockesque peace-signs and declarations of love to

Marley, Morrison and Hendrix. Strumming a sad guitar on a Royal Enfield is a soap-dodger with a spliff between his walrus and soul-patch.

The inside of the tent presents a number of string-cots, arranged head-to-tail-to-head-to-tail along the circumference. Like a seer in the middle is a large samovar on legs, surrounded by concentric rings of chairs. A Nepali man at a counter by the entrance is rolling out and simultaneously preparing chapatis on a gas range; a woman with a blissful smile nearby is counting (why?) chapatis already stacked in a tall pile; another man at the other end is chopping a pile of onions. The Nepali man asks if we have come for the rave party. If so, we are early.

'For something to eat, actually,' I reply.

'Anything,' beams the lady looking up from the chapatis. 'Anything you like. Chapati, omelette, bread butter cornflakes, mil-tee-kofi, anything, even bed to slee and res.'

'Omelettes and chapatis will be just fine. And tea for him and a coffee for me. Thank you. We'll wait outside. Okay?'

'Okay, thank you,' she replies. We step outside.

The soap-dodger plays an elaborate riff and gives the sad guitar a rest.

'Good show,' says Man. The man throws him a look of intense hatred.

Another soap-dodger has cycled up, meanwhile. This one inscribes a figure-of-eight in front of the tent before pedalling uphill, calf muscles straining.

'Good show!' yells Man.

'You know,' I say. 'I'd think twice before dispensing good shows like blessings to these chaps.'

'Why? I'm encouraging them.'

'If someone were to good show to me in that poncy way, I'd probably break their fingers.'

'See, that's the difference. Not everyone has grouch for their middle name.'

I smile. 'Like that chap on Chang La, you mean? Remember?'

'He *waved* in acknowledgement; groucho imagined something else.'

'Sure. Oh good. Finally.'

The smiling lady has popped out of the tent with our chapatis and omelettes, tea and coffee.

'Good show, dear lady. Thank you very kindly.'

I pretend I'm not here and make a roll of my omelette and chapati. The coffee is scalding and very sweet. Bliss.

'Anything else, gentleman?' the lady giggles.

'Good show! Another round of these please,' says Man. In time, more Royal Enfields arrive up the hill. Good show, says Man to the new arrivals. They give us a wide berth and enter the tent.

'Come join inside,' says the happy lady in an earnest sort of way, but neither of us is feeling adventurous at this stage. An hour later, at Jispa, we find a hotel and pass out for the night.

21

The Tibetan word *rohtang* translates to 'pile of corpses'. It lends itself to the name for a La on the Pir Pinjal Range between the Lahaul-Spiti and Kullu-Parvati valleys of Himachal Pradesh; the pass had begun life as a caravan trail connecting the two sides.

Snowbound for close to eight months, Rohtang La reopens each year around late May and June. Between then and late October or November when it goes back into hibernation, the road witnesses heavy traffic, primarily by way of military convoys proceeding to Ladakh. But the pass is also the sole conduit for civilian vehicles entering Ladakh from the Manali–Leh Road and exiting, as we are, via the same road. Apprehensions that Rohtang may not yet be open for the Season had been laid to rest earlier this morning at Keylong where we had stopped for a full-tank of fuel; two days earlier, and we would have been stuck at any of the tented shanties before the pass, waiting indefinitely for the all-clear. It is 10.20 a.m. when we commence the ascent.

At 13,051 feet and 11.20 a.m., the summit is pristine under the gracious sky. No small wonder that this ethereal place has long been celebrated on celluloid as a song-sequence dreamscape, is rivalled only by Shimla as a honeymooner's cliché, remains the evergreen thrill-seeker's favourite nightmare, and is even touted as India's answer to Aspen even if there are no conifers or log cabins to clutter this utter inimitable innocent blankness. But look again.

I spy with my bleary eye a set of pylons, ski-lifts perhaps, where a snowfield has curved like a sleeping swan's neck. A clutch of tiny figures seems to be tobogganing there; it's hard to tell for the glare. The road inscribes a smooth line up a dollop and onto the other side. The sight below elicits a synchronized scream from Man and me.

The downhill stretch is lined on both sides with civilian vehicles of every type, parked bumper-to-bumper, downslope and upslope, with just enough room for more of their kind to course up and down in between. There must be well over a thousand cars, SUVs, buses and vans in all with hundreds of motorbikes, both stationary and crawling. The slopes on either side have erupted a rash of bodies – millions, a veritable Juhu-Chowpatty meets Puri-Rath Yatra, transposed to the snowfields for a spot of Sunday excitement. There's no turning around and certainly not off-road; a red behemoth is breathing down our backs, nudging us on with short sharp yarps. Before we know it, we are one with the queue inching downhill, with inches to spare between the one coming uphill. Just when it couldn't get any worse, something, somewhere, brings the queues to a standstill. The road at once turns into four lines of motionless vehicles, with only the bikers weaving out and in. The hatchback in front of us is farting black. We roll up our windows and watch, speechless.

The holidaymakers on the slopes have come dressed for the Arctic. For those that haven't, a number of resourceful types have installed kiosks of gumboots, sunhats, jumpsuits and faux-fur capes to rent. Also in attendance are vendors of helium-balloons, cotton candy, popcorn, bottled water, fried foods, *chai-garam* and fizzy-drinks. There are no dustbins, but animals aplenty: moth-eaten ponies with tatty saddles and harnesses, and viscose teddy bears and penguins and bunnies in lurid pinks, greens and blues. A jumpsuited man near us struggles with the zipper of another man, half-in and half-out of an ill-fitting jumpsuit. Other men are wandering aimlessly about with vacant expressions. A young woman primps past in leopard spots and dominatrix boots. An elderly couple stands shell-shocked, either by AMS or in surprise at where they have landed. There's no shortage of honeymooners (identifiable by the poses they strike in hired Himachali-trad), professional photographers, children and babes in the arms of zombified mothers. And everywhere in the guck that once was driven-white are frozen streaks of yellow where ponies and humans have emptied their bladders. Oddly, there isn't a single smile in sight. Nor, for that matter, a red-cross sign. I wonder, idly, morbidly, what would happen if Pir Pinjal were to shrug, or if the wind were to change, or the sky get thunderous.

The hatchback in front has just been given a signal to move by a harried marshal in khaki. The man, armed with a baton and a walkie, taps on Man's window to say it's worse lower down, drive slow and don't overtake.

The nightmare doesn't end for another hour and a half, so we inch past an earth-mover that has cleared the road of a landslide, through another clog-up ahead, past hundreds more vehicles going uphill, under a frightening overhang where the road becomes a single-lane ledge over a ravine. It is 1.20 p.m. when we are out in the clear, looping easily down through montane grassland first, and then forests of conifer followed by orchards of apple. Someday, plans for a tunnel through Pir Pinjal will shimmy off the drawing board and shoot under the mountain. It probably will live up to its promise of easing congestion. Until then, the sole link between the valleys will remain a disaster waiting to happen.

Kullu, 4 p.m. The bungalow on a tree-filled knoll is early twentieth century in architecture and spirit. A wave of goodness draws us through the doorway in a warm embrace. The source that has led us to this once-private house had also furnished a little-known detail. The Mahatma had stayed here – long before its present incarnation as the Silver Moon Hotel.

Behind glazed double-doors, our high-ceilinged suite is decorated with framed prints of Roerich mountainscapes; the redoubtable Russian artist (1874–1947) had spent the evening of his life in the little town of Naggar nearby. The bathroom has a bath with old brass faucets that gurgle and burp to yield hot jets. The windows of the dressing room overlook a patch of the garden round the side of the building where a holy man in purple silk is addressing a small but rapt audience.

Afternoon tea, on the front lawn, appears in white chinaware. The borders are thriving with hollyhocks and poppies and sunbirds and butterflies. We've brought down our binoculars; the opposite hillside is dotted with old bungaloid buildings, calm in their wrap of coniferous trees. The discourse in the side garden has ended. The holy man is seen off to his sedan and the gathering thins. Shortly, a colourless couple and a child occupy a table near ours and order high tea. The child frightens away the birds and mangles a butterfly. This makes me livid. The parents of the child get livid that I'm livid. But I'm not about to let anyone or anything ruin my evening. Having glowered those people into silence, Man and I proceed to enjoy our chicken sandwiches and tea and then walk briskly up and down the tree-lined drive until it gets nippy and the light starts to fade. Tomorrow, very early, we must check out of the Silver Moon and begin our descent to the North Indian plains.

It is the start of an eight-hour long drive. It finds Man in exceptionally high spirits, whistling tuneless melodies to the pine-scented air. The luscious hill road is punctuated with cautionary signs.

Alert always
Drive do not fly
Anytime is safe time
I'm curvaceous go slow
I love you but not so fast
After wiskey driving is risky
Lower your gear curve is near
Overspeed is knife that cuts life
Safety on roads = safe tea at home
If you are married divorce the speed
Kashmir to Kanyakumari India is One

There are more along the same lines but those are the best. Soon, there is little of worth to commit to memory or render in ink. It is late in the evening when we reach Delhi and Safdarjung Enclave.

The morning is balmy. The Colonel's health had given Man's mum a bit of a scare on the precise day that we were at Pang Gong. He's back in form again. 'Tell me about the colours,' he says.

Later, Man takes him and the nurse out for a drive. When they return an hour later from topping-up P.Singh, Man informs me that we won't be leaving tomorrow as planned: dad would like us to stay another day. It makes perfect sense. I make myself scarce for the rest of the day – first for beers and lunch at a chocolatiere friend's, moving on for more beers and dinner at a designer friend's. It is almost 2 a.m. when I am delivered home by other friends. Man's stayed up to let me in.

'Happy birthday,' I say and dive into bed.

It is lunchtime the next day when I surface. That evening – our last evening en famille – Man cuts a fruitcake that has survived a long drive in Redbox as well as a gifting spree at Tso Moriri.

The next two days are a blur – the mind's way, no doubt, of blanking out all but the most relevant details. We do break journey in Rajasthan, in Bundi. It reinforces my opinion that some places must never be revisited, and even if they are, not as part of a different experience. The eighteenth-century palace on the hill has crumbled some more in the nine years that have elapsed since a previous visit; its irreparable, inimitable inner fabric of murals have further deteriorated. At Ellora Maharashtra (via Indore in Madhya Pradesh), the following evening, I don't attempt a revisit of a ninth-century rock-cut marvel, a short distance from our hotel.

The tempo of the last day of the journey is set, post-breakfast, by an incident on the trafficless road out of Ellora. The police vehicle is parked under a tree at a gentle curve. Its uniformed driver, standing outside, flags us to a standstill. Unlike their Western counterparts who saunter up to the vehicle they have stopped, Indian cops remain in their vehicles and, from their window, issue whatever it is they must charge one with.

The oily number in this police vehicle is not too pleased to find Man's driving licence and P.Singh's documents are all in order. Because it would be dull of him to let us proceed, he decides that P.Singh's emission-test certificate, issued in Karnataka, does not meet the pollution-control standards of Maharashtra. For this, he must levy a fine of Rs 500.

'Nonsense,' I snort.

'Don't you call me nonsense,' he snarls. 'Five hundred now, or I will seize all your documents. And then we'll see who is nonsense.'

Much against my will, I extricate a crisp note of said denomination and hand it to the swine. In exchange, he hands Man back all of the documents, ascertains the currency is not counterfeit, and folds it deftly into a breast pocket.

'I'd like a receipt for that,' I say.

'A receipt? Be grateful I didn't fine you one thousand,' he sneers. His driver, watching through the other window, contributes a wink. The dashboard of their mobile-office is done up as a shrine to Ganesha and Shirdi Baba.

'You ought to be ashamed,' I say. 'Barefaced robbery in full view of divinity.'

'Government work is god's work,' the man guffaws. 'Now *chalo*.'

I am still bristling when we crawl out of Aurangabad. The weather that has stayed placid until now undergoes a slight change in mood. The light, mid-morning drizzle stays with us for well over an hour. By the time we enter Bijapur, North Karnataka, early afternoon, it has started to bucket down with no sign of letting up. An eight-lane highway soon turns into a four-lane one, and then a two-lane ribbon of slush, lumbering with tarp-covered trucks and inter-state buses and oncoming traffic with headlights blazing. At Hospet, Central Deccan, a toppled truck has brought all traffic to a standstill in the rain for what appears to be a kilometre, with helpful locals walking up and down selling onion-fritters and tea from under their umbrellas. It is 5.30 p.m. by the time the roadblock is cleared and the dead taken away.

On a good day, the drive from Hospet to Bangalore takes a little over five hours to complete. Today is not one of those days, so Man takes the home stretch, as it were, in sheets of monsoon and complete focus on the wretched scarred cratered highway. His nerves are utterly frazzled but he is not letting on. Not tonight. Not ever, come to think of it.

It is still coming down when we stop, at 1.15 a.m., in the portico of an establishment, second-home, at which I've decided to stay the next couple of days, take stock, get laundry done, loll about, pretend I am still away. P.Singh's odometer reads 031375. We've done 8,395 kilometres since we set out on the eighteenth of May – all of it without a single mechanical glitch or flat.

'Talk soon,' says Man. They'll be home and dry in under ten minutes.

'Talk soon.'

As P.Singh's taillights wink and vanish into the rain, something tells me this journey is not quite over. Self-fulfilling prophecy. A little under a year from now, I'll find myself back in Ladakh.

22

6.35 a.m. It is a remarkably short flight of sixty minutes out of Delhi. The stewardesses in poppy-red have cleared away the snack-trays; we are half an hour from touchdown in Leh. With me in Seat 07A is Lama Anagarika Govinda, né, 1898, Ernst Lothar Hoffman. Books have a way of claiming their readers; the Lama's was recommended, over a year ago, by a friend in Germany and winged in as a timely gift, two days ago from a friend in Texas. I open *The Way of The White Clouds* at random for my first taste of it.

The page yields a ponderous meditation – no other word for it – on happy chance, coincidence and serendipity. But what the Lama sets forth in a hundred-and-six words, I have summarised in six. It's too early in the day for high philosophy; still, I read the passage twice for its subtle complexities, and then shut the book and tuck it away.

A great invisible force, meanwhile, has reached into the cabin and smothered the ambient hiss of fans and soft belch of seats, the cold clink of seatbelts, the rustle of newsprint, the coughs and sniffs and nameless whirrs and clicks – everything – to that particular, absolute, silence when everything feels like a marble slab. A slight dip and tilt causes a blinding gold flare to break through the windows, east, across the aisle and touch the tops of seats and sleeping heads, dart to the front and dive between the curtains there. A judder and a whine; the cabin lights die; the seatbelt-signs beep twice and blink. I look out of my window, west.

There is nothing to be seen. We are motionless, suspended in an opaque morass of grey. The minutes crawl; the substance releases its grip and we are sailing, once again, above a calmness of white. A blip, also white, materialises from beneath and rips through like a knife-point to reveal all of itself and more peaks – all of them ruched, blue-shadowed and shot through with white-gold.

The bare lower ranges beyond, scarred with diagonals of ochre, mauve, rose and black, are herding inexorably onto a broad flat valley. The ground there is dotted with chortens like lost sheep. The plane inscribes a wide arc and begins its descent. A monastery on an outcrop gazes out towards the airport named for a Rinpoche. We make a velvet landing. Outside, at 10,682 feet, the temperature is 12°C.

'Julley, Vikram le. Khamzang in-a le?'

The correct response to which inquiry would be: 'Julley, Yangchan le. Khamzang in le. Nyereng khamzang in-a le?'

'Khamzang in le. Julley.'

We are attempting, at my request, a small departure from our lingua franca of Hindi-English into the light aspirates and sibilants of Ladakhi with its ad hoc sprinklings of the honorific suffix. I am yet to hear this delightfully cadenced language in anything other than a polite decibel level. To speak louder than one's interlocutors is held, in these parts, to be a sign of certain boorishness. Said credo probably has more to do with reserving one's breath for better things in such thin air. Whatever its source, it suits me perfectly.

'And you, Wangial le?' I pose in my usual dulcet voice, 'Khamzang in-a le, today?'

'Khamzang, julley, Vikram le,' he replies, indicating my cup of butter tea with a courtly flourish: 'Don le. Solja don le.'

'Ot julley,' I reply, taking a sip and committing *don* and *solja* to memory.

It's my second morning at the Gangba homestead. Their suggestion, yesterday, that I acclimatized fully before wandering off anywhere had translated to a marathon sleep-in. We haven't, as a result, had a chance to catch up on news and happenings. I've also missed Jigmet who had stopped by last evening, found me asleep, and had threatened to return after work this evening.

I am crosslegged now on a divan in the glass-room, tucking into a warm khambir half-slathered with butter and honey. Very little has changed here in the year that has whizzed by. Little Tsering Wangmo – an inch taller perhaps and still a brat – has been packed off to school with a satchel as big as herself. Ama le, Wangial's mum, is saying her prayer beads over the new curls of green in the vegetable beds. The one addition to the family, a bundle of canine black named Tommy, is lying on his back in a rectangle of sunlight. A gust of sparrows descends into the willow hedges to hold a conference. Yangchan and Wangial pour some tea for themselves and sit facing me. Their expressions are expectant.

Over the following two weeks, I begin, I intend to sleep, take long walks and put in a spot of work on a book I am writing. It would be nice to steal your recipe for chu-tagie to include in it.

Is it a cookbook that you are writing?

A book about last year's journey. Food, you could say, is an ingredient.

When will it be ready?

I have no idea. But most of it is in here in raw form if you wish to sample it.

They open the cherry-red folder on the chogtse. It is hard to tell what they're thinking as they work their way through the typescript, first page to last, pausing now and again to mutter softly between themselves, and then returning to and dwelling at length over our first meeting. How easy it has been to write about people I have only briefly met. How odd it must feel to be reading about themselves. What if the chogtse, as it were, were turned this instant. I suddenly feel a little queasy.

'Do you think I have an "anxious expression"?' Yangchan asks Wangial, pulling a funny face.

'You certainly do,' he laughs. 'And look, Vikram le is looking anxious as well.'

'Oof! I knew from the start he was up to no good. Looking here, looking there, thinking we didn't notice, scribbling away in that little notebook. Now we know why.'

'It didn't exactly begin that way,' I protest. 'I was minding my business, agonizing over something entirely different, until that morning on Khardung La with your thermos of kahwa. For which, once again, many thanks.'

'Ah julley. You can stop looking anxious, Vikram le. I shall ply you with as much kahwa as you desire so that you may continue to write about katangputits and khambir. But do tell us: how is Manoj le? Such a *shareef aadmi*, so quiet and polite. Did he not wish to visit us again?'

'Hugely disappointed that he couldn't,' I reply, making a mental note to convey aforementioned perception to its object. 'You see, he was so energized by his long drive that he flung himself headlong into a new job shortly after we got back. And so, in addition to being a responsible son, spouse, parent and pal, he now also holds the keys to the treasury of a large company. Which technically means he's stuck for life. He sends you his warmest wishes; he is in Delhi as we speak.'

'Does he no longer live in Bangalore?'

'No; it's just that he travels up whenever he can to spend a couple of days with his mother.'

Yangchan seems to have picked up a nuance somewhere: 'Is everyone well?'

'As well as they can be under the circumstances,' I reply. I then inform them that Man had lost his father in April.

We are silent for a long moment. My thoughts drift all over the past and present. The pink-gold copperware in the langs before me, the rocking chair in Delhi, magpies arguing in the poplar trees, monochrome photographs, gulls alighting, a paintbrush rolled under a chogtse, the lake.

The moment passes. A breeze wanders indoors muttering to itself. I look up, and cannot help but smile.

Like an absent-minded djinn in burgundy velvet, Ama le enters the glass-room in a cloud of incense billowing from the censer in her hands.

Lama Anagarika's *Way of the White Clouds* has set me on the hunt for a book by one Alexandra David-Néel.

An Orientalist and explorer of Belgian-French extraction, Mme David-Néel had tramped all over Tibet during the opening decades of the twentieth century, twice meeting the thirteenth Dalai Lama in 1912 – she was the first European woman ever to be granted audience – and doggedly pursuing a study of Buddhism with teachers as diverse as bandits on high passes and cave-dwelling hermits.

In 1924, aged fifty-six, this redoubtable character notched another first: she sneaked in, incognito, disguised as a pilgrim into the Forbidden City, which was technically off bounds to non-Tibetans. She spent two months in Lhasa, undetected, and left, undetected, to continue her wanderings in the Himalayas. A decade later, she published a memoir of her experiences of levitating monks and the like, as well as mundane aspects of monastic life, told with a magpie-eye for detail and rare warmth and wit. The work and its author had clearly exerted a profound influence on Lama Anagarika; he may have carried the book on his travels in Tibet of the late 1940s. If there's one place in the immediate neighbourhood where I might, just might, find a copy, it would have to be the Leh-Ling Bookshop on Market Road.

The last time I was here, Man and I had gifted ourselves a volume each of Janet Rizvi's *Ladakh*. The shop has just opened for the day and the apple-cheeked proprietress, bobbing about with a duster, chirrups a bright julley. There are two other customers – one of them browsing the floor-to-ceiling shelves like a melancholy giraffe, his squarer companion selecting postcards from an extensive countertop display. I give the shelves a close inspection, don't find what I'm looking for, resist the lure of a monumental monograph on the Alchi temples, and only then interrupt Mme Apple.

'Ha le,' she smiles, locating a paperback that has been rubbing spines all along with fine art and philosophy. 'Same author and book, but reprint with different title.'

I can hardly believe my luck and express as much – perhaps a tad too loudly, for the giraffe and the groundhog exchange a glance and a sneer. But never mind them. In its current incarnation, the cover of David-Néel's *With Mystics and Magicians in Tibet* carries a less-swashbuckling title floated in grey over a grey-and-white photograph of the Potala Palace, all of it enlivened by the hot-pink of the blurb and the author's name. As I am wont to with any new book, I open *Magic & Mystery in Tibet* at random:

> A much appreciated intermission cuts the long service: tea is brought in steaming hot, flavoured with butter and salt, according to the Tibetan taste. It is carried in large wooden buckets whose bearer walks along the rows. Each *trapa* produces his own bowl, kept till then under his vest next to

> his skin. The bowls are a special pattern which vary according to the sects. No china or silver ornamented bowls are allowed at the assembly. The highest dignitaries must use a plain wooden one. Yet even that rule, meant as a symbolic remembrance of the renunciation and poverty enjoyed by the original Buddhist discipline, is avoided by the austere lamas. The bowl of the richest among them is truly made of wood, but some of these wooden utensils, made of special timbers out of the excrescences that grow on the trunks of certain trees, are highly prized and may cost as much as the equivalent of £6 in local currency.

I'm hooked. The lead up to the paragraph is an almost cinematic account, c. 1930, of a congregation of monks and little novices assembled for prayers in the dhukhang of a Tibetan gompa; the interior is swoony with smells and sounds, flickering lamps and strange shadows. An interlude, and out come the tea bowls. There's an immediacy to this voice – a perfect foil for the ponderous tones that had led me to it. I make my purchase – it is their last copy – and hurry outside.

I slow down. Round the corner, the other length of Market Road is going about life at its signature pace. The motionless queues of soldiers and backpackers outside the ATMs of the State Bank of India; the rakish Kashmiri tradesmen, upping the shutters of their souvenir shops between sizing up the passers-by; the Ladakhi biddies rolling with prayer beads, manis and mantras into the courtyard of Chokang Vihara; the Tibetan refugees from Choglamsar arranging their merchandise of silver and semi-precious on their trestle-table shop-tops; the zhankeys, like discarded sackcloths, oblivious to everything under the sharpening morning. From a folding chair by the tree outside the Vihara, a vaguely aristocratic figure in a deep-coral jacket is watching his world go by with a stern expression and a cup of tea. It is my old friend, the purveyor of fine carpets.

'Good morning, Mr Wangnoo.'

He looks up with a frown which slowly dissolves to a smile.

'Good morning, sir,' he says, rising to his feet and taking my hand. 'I remember; you purchased a kilim from me last year. What a pleasure to see you again. When did you arrive?'

'Guilty and likewise. It's been three days, I think; possibly four. I must stop by at the shop one of these days.'

He laughs and taps the side of his nose: 'Ah. You are always welcome. Please come by any time you wish.'

And so, over cups of kahwa in Hassan Wangnoo's shop, I spend a very pleasant morning looking at kilims.

We'd made up a little rhyme the other afternoon and the name has stuck:

Little Miss Gangba sat in the glass-room
eating her tsampa and apricot stew.
Along came a dzo and sat down beside her
so Miss Gangba gobbled him up too.

This afternoon is a little different. Tsering Wangmo has changed out of her school uniform into an eclectic layering of knits and voiles. A set of pigments, glistening wetly in their thimble-like containers, is arranged before the child. In goes the brush into one of the colours and from it directly onto a page. A smear, and the brush takes a sip from a glass of mocha water, dives into a different colour, back onto the paper, another smear, back into the water, into the next colour, smear-smear, in and out, in and out, through the whole range.

With each foray of her brush, Tsering's frown of concentration darkens into a scowl of frustration. If only she were enjoying this, I'd stay a mute observer; I cannot bear it a moment longer. What I am itching to do might put her off paints forever, or she might create a timeless work of art. Whatever the outcome, meddle I must.

'Are you having fun, Miss Gangba?'

'No. I am trying to make a colour.'

'What colour would that be?'

'Any colour.'

'D'you know,' I say with studied indifference. 'with just three of those colours, you can have masses of fun making many, many different colours?'

Her response is prompt: 'How?'

'Would you like to give it a shot?'

She nods, sending her pigtail bouncing.

'But first, we'll need a clean brush, four glasses of clean water and three saucers. If you can get those organized in three minutes, we can get started.'

Over the next three quarters of an hour, little Miss Gangba has an introduction to the not-so-mysterious ways of colour; her brush too must be ecstatic. Primary-red combines with primary-yellow to yield orange. Yellow and blue turn bright cucumber. Blue plus red becomes brinjal. It's a short step from the secondaries into the tertiaries and onwards into weirder combinations. Two small diversions, via a dab of white, a dab of black, take her into the world of tints and shades. The best part is that we can assign any name we wish: from lama and saffron to puce, mud and vomit. There's no stopping the child; I am inordinately pleased to have created a fiend.

Because it is summer, the days are balmy and long and the nights nippy and short. I've been rising at four every morning to a pre-dawn rehearsal of birdsong, winging from the gully of boulders that defines the eastern boundary of the acreage. Within half-an-hour, the light is just right for stepping outdoors, onwards up the Upper Tukcha Road, and around the still sleeping Market Road. By the time I'm back, maybe an hour later, the rest of the household has begun its day.

This morning, the birds are muffled by the sound of water, somewhere between full-spate and trickle, from the general direction of the gully. It trails me all the way to the main gates of the homestead where it changes its mind and heads back towards the house. I let myself out into complete silence. The secret to prolonging these outings, and also to saving my breath in the thin air is to shorten my stride and, in the manner of the locals, to take everything at an amble.

There is usually someone or the other to be encountered at this hour along the long and narrow winding road. The brigadier (I'm certain he is one) with the curt nod and swagger stick. The somnambulistic dzo with the rope through his nostrils. The little old lady with the tea-cosy bonnet and rolling duckwalk.

The redstarts hopping about on the whitewashed stone walls. The same pair of magpies like finials to the tarchoks in the roof of a house. The dinky cows where the road curves past an apricot grove. The romantic in the plum beret who, like me, likes to stop and look. His usual spot is the bridge under the poplars. Mine is at a length of low wall further up the road for an uninterrupted parallel sweep of the Stok Range.

I've come to look forward to my daily fix of this view – once in the morning and then again in the evening when the snowpeaks start to alter. It must be this particular combination of air and light, the measured pace of life in this neighbourhood, the neat little houses with their neat grids of fenestration and rambling rose bushes, the Old Palace behind me and these mountains in front. Each time I stop here, I find myself lulled into a state of light-headed calm.

In the little windows of clarity that open during these moments, I run an inventory of items of personal significance. People; choices; that sort of thing. Other times are for appreciating how little one needs in order to quietly chug along. Too much introspection of this nature, and I'll be sporting a halo and floating, like some David-Néel item, virtuously up and down the road. Most times, therefore, are for staring at the horizon and emptying my head of similes and semi-colons.

This morning, a man and a woman are standing, quite motionless, in the barley field over the wall. Both are armed with long-handled shovels. Perhaps they are waiting for something, a crop-raider perhaps. I stop at my usual spot.

The man bids a soft julley. The woman, further away, lifts a hand in greeting. The sun, tickling the snowpeaks in the distance, is yet to touch the barley. Abruptly, to some unspoken cue, the pair works the ground briefly with the shovels and then pauses for a full minute. When they move, it is to take a few steps backwards and sideways and pause once again. It's an odd little ballet of two silent silhouettes. I lean forward over the wall; it takes a moment to work out what they are doing.

The ground to one side is darkly wet in the neat narrow rectangles of new barley. The water spreads like a stain as the couple works: opening little gaps in the sides of the beds and scratching furrows in the dry earth to help the water along. The moment one bed is sufficiently soaked, the inflow is staunched with a quick shovelful of earth and a gap opened into the neighbouring bed – and onwards in the same way along the length of the acreage.

About two acres have been watered; an almost equal area remains to be irrigated. The main water source is a channel running alongside the lane, from which a narrower channel has been led under the wall and into the field.

'How long have you been at it?' I call out to the man.

'Since 3 a.m.,' he replies.

What I'm witnessing is an age-old irrigation technique which I'd first seen in Nubra last year. Jigmet had explained the associated water-sharing tradition, endemic to these parts where water is precious. Once a week in summer, glacial melt was released from a reservoir to different parts of a town or a village based on a pre-determined rota. There was no charge for drawing the water into the fields from the main feeder channels. Each homestead utilized only as much as it required, and only during the hours allotted to them. There was little chance of wastage or misuse: no one would wilfully cause their neighbours' crops to perish.

'We hear you are from Bangalore,' says the man, leaning over his shovel.

'That is correct.'

'How do your people water their fields?'

'We rely almost entirely on the monsoon,' I reply.

He laughs: 'Ah yes, the monsoon. If it ever rained that way here, it would not be very good.'

'And our winters are unlike the ones you experience.'

'How long are you staying with the Gangbas? We see you here everyday. Sometimes twice.'

'Another ten days.'

'Very good. Julley.'

'Julley.'

I stay and watch until the whole expanse gets watered. Shovel-pause, shovel-pause. It must be well past seven by the time they finish. The man walks up to the far end of the wall where he blocks the inlet with a sandbag. Another wave and a julley, and the couple moves slowly towards a house lower down the acreage.

'You've been away longer than usual?' says Wangial when I get back.

'I was watching the barley being watered up the road,' I tell him.

'It is our turn in a couple of days,' he says, handing me my mug of coffee. 'We meant to ask: would you mind taking over the kitchen then?'

It is a quiet afternoon outside the café in the square at the top of Upper Tukcha Road. A breeze teases the hems of the gingham tablecloths. To celebrate a ruthless edit of the typescript – I won't have to look at it again for a while – I'm treating myself to a cigarette, coffee and a wedge of lemon cheesecake. The first is a guilty secret. The cheesecake is generously proportioned and zesty. The coffee, not instant, arrives in a French press. I make a meditation of the plunger so the aroma and liquor lift darkly clear garnet. I sit back and shut my eyes. My caffeine-nicotine buzz is short-lived.

The 4x4 taxi has turned into the road in a high gear, scattering pedestrians and scraping the edge of the square as it brakes. The driver's door flies open to emit a frazzled young Ladakhi. He jumps to the terrace but isn't quick enough for two other figures spat out by the SUV. They are the common variety of Indian male – the sort that wouldn't merit a glance under normal circumstances.

The older of the two makes a grab for the driver's jacket, connects, and pulls himself onto the terrace, simultaneously causing the latter to overbalance. The younger, sprung from the same lumpen genes, joins in to rain blows on the youth, aiming a kick to his side before dragging and pushing him across the terrace. The spectacle has drawn a small gathering that looks too stunned to intervene. Anywhere else, the outsiders – for that's what these are – would have been promptly thrashed to within an inch of their lives. Luckily for them, crudeness in any form is an alien concept to the Ladakhi temperament; their victim makes no move to defend himself or to retaliate. 'STOP THAT,' I bellow from my table, remembering, too late, that standoff on Baralacha La with a different SUV.

The louts swing round to see who dared oppose them. The young man seizes the chance to break free and vanishes. I brace myself for whatever must happen.

The younger of the two takes a step in my direction but – it has to be my RayBans and week-old stubble – changes his mind to instead spit a mother-sister expletive and a gob of phlegm. Senior pulls Junior back; they turn and saunter into one of the travel agencies around the terrace. The bystanders surge as one to gather outside, craning their necks to catch the action inside. Several minutes tick by. I sip my coffee and assume an air of lordly nonchalance.

Shortly, the crush makes way for the pair to emerge. Without looking left or right, they smirk their way down to the taxi which, I only now notice, is packed with blank-faced women and children. A different Ladakhi, meanwhile, has jumped behind the wheel and reverses the party up and out of the Upper Tukcha Road. The moment they vanish, the browbeaten youth creeps out from a different travel agent's. He's given a backslapping reception and herded by his mates towards the café.

'Julley,' he says, pulling up a chair at the table next to mine, 'Thank you.' The side of his face has gone purple-blue.

'Anytime,' I reply. 'What was all that about?'

'Indian tourists,' he shrugs. 'Usual problem. They wanted refund.'

'Boss has refunded 50 per cent,' grins one of the other men.

Turns out the party had made a day trip, of all moronic things, to Pang Gong – setting out from their hotel later than scheduled. I do a quick calculation: about four hours to get there, even at a modest pace, up and down Chang La, and four hours for the return. Racing to and fro couldn't have been much fun for anyone.

'What did they do there?'

'Usual thing. Take photos, eat, make lots of noise, maximum thirty minutes. One lady became sick in Chang La top during return trip. Luckily road was clear both ways today so we reached down quick. She is okay but they said everything is my fault.'

'Was that why they beat you up?'

He frowns and inspects his fingernails. 'Main reason was because seedy got stuck.'

I must look incredibly stupid.

He laughs. 'This year they all bring Bollywood seedy for going to Pang Gong lake. Sometimes they like to dance. It is ugly to see. Today when seedy stopped and did not come out, they started to abuse saying that I have done it purposely to spoil their time. That fat man used some very bad language. In front of ladies and children. No self-respect.'

'You should've left them behind on Chang La.'

It's lost on him. 'How can I do that?'

Granted, his options are limited. I try one for potential, more to cheer him up a bit. 'Quite simple. The next time something like that happens, chuck out their things, lock yourself in, drive. It isn't their vehicle. No one can accuse you of theft.'

'I will lose my job if I do that.'

'You don't mind being hit, then? Tomorrow, it could be something else.'

'But it is bad if I show anger in return. They are guests. They must go with good impression of Ladakhi culture. Otherwise it will be bad for us, for business.'

Those yokels wouldn't know culture if it stared them in the eye. I feel an intense wave of annoyance at this pious self-sacrificing whine. Sit long enough on a fence and all you get is barbed wire up your backside.

'Good luck to you all.' I settle my bill and leave.

My mobile phone connection that had remained dead through our drive last year has miraculously remained serviceable since the morning I landed. I haven't much use for it, aside from the occasional text message; the phone itself has become a device for telling the time. It rings while I'm on my afternoon fix of kahwa and kilims.

It is Sreya: 'We know you're working and really don't want to bother you, but Yogi and I were wondering, *if* you can and if it isn't *too* much of a pain, will you bring us a kilim?'

'You're in luck,' I say. 'I'm standing on just the one.'

'What?'

'A kilim.'

'Liar.'

'I'm at the carpet place,' I say, lowering my voice. 'You couldn't have called at a better time. I've been eyeing it the last fifteen minutes. Large enough to roll in a fat Cleopatra, so I'm not sure how I'll lug it back.'

'It can be couriered,' says Mr Wangnoo discreetly behind me. The hall must host an echo.

'It can be couriered,' I say down the mobile. And that settles that.

On the walk back, I surprise Man in his air-conditioned office from my spot by the wall, expressly to paint him a scene of the peaks changing from vanilla to butterscotch with a marbling of strawberry. From the silence at the other end, I can tell he can do with a hint of Leh-afternoon incense, the sparrows cheep-cheeping in the willows – here, listen – and the children racing on cycles singing julley-julley.

'Sadist. Anything else?'

'That's all for now. Swing by later.'

'Have you ever been up to see the palace, Vikram le?'

'No. I haven't.'

'You have been up to the Shanti Stupa, surely?'

'Nope; neither the stupa nor the palace.'

'How can that be? The views from there are very fine.'

'Watching people up-close is a lot more entertaining.'

'Stop watching and give us a hand,' laughs Wangial.

'Back in a minute,' I wave.

Husband and wife have been tending the barley since 4 a.m., with Tommy and a thermos of solja for company. Shanti Stupa, watching over us from the hillock nearby, is dazzling now in the mid-morning light. Beyond it, clear skies over a shoulder of Khardung La, the fine line that is the Highest Motorable Pass in the World visible, seen quite distinctly, from this distance.

Kitchen duties today, so I've just returned from the market with two dressed chickens: frozen, not fresh-cut, in compliance with some peculiar logic whereby it is fine to partake of that which one hasn't actively rendered lifeless (or been party to rendering lifeless) and which bears little resemblance to its original, clucking or bleating self. I leave the plasticy, presumably soulless, things to thaw in the kitchen sink and return to the barley fields.

The watered areas are gloopy and I must watch where I step. Wangial hands me his shovel. In my very first go at it, I make a hash of the inlet into a bed, causing the water to flood, not flow. Yangchan is quick to control the mess with a deft clod of earth to the botched opening. I am allowed three more attempts before Wangial politely reclaims the shovel.

They pause to do a quick assessment of how much remains to be irrigated. This whole business of grid-lines and sequence is a lot more strategic than I had imagined, with barely a second between the closing of one inlet and the opening, diagonally across, of the next. The barley itself, evenly spaced, is planted in diagonals, with the earth lightly furrowed between the lines.

'All this must appear quite different from South Indian paddy fields,' remarks Yangchan.

'We just flood 'em,' I say, 'No need there for shovels and embankments.'

'No shovels needed for that side,' says Wangial pointing to the edge of the field, 'When we're done here, we'll let the water flow through the *ol* until 4 p.m.'

I walk over for a look.

The lower terrace is lush with lucerne – cattle-feed, when dry – between a stand of pencil-thin poplars. To the left, defining

Magic carpet

Tso Moriri

Tso Kar

Kiangs near Tso Kar

Dust devil, Moore Plains

Irises, Leh

Accoutrements of prayer, Hemis dhukhang

Butter lamps and murals, Hemis dhukhang

The monk, Hemis gompa

Julley! katangputit

the southern boundary of the homestead, the orchard of apricot and apple marches towards the rear façade of the house. A slight movement in the trees flashes a wink of gold and brick-red. 'I'll see you both later,' I say, and make my way down to the trees.

Sonam Choskit Gangba, Ama le to everyone, stopped trudging up to Market Road with her *tsepo* of vegetables since that time she felt more than a little wobbly on the walk back. Nothing serious, the *amchi* had told Wangial. Your mother is strong as a drimo. She just needs to take it easy.

And so, although she misses the gossip, the laughter and the people-watching – the veg were only an excuse for an outing – Ama le is happy enough these days to potter around the acreage, praying for it and its permanent and transient residents. Excursions beyond the gates are limited mainly to Chokhang Vihara, with a detour to one of her daughters' nearby. She has a way of referring to herself in the third-person, as though she were the mouthpiece of an invisible twin.

Ama le is now looking forward, she says from her boulder under an apricot tree, to visiting the Nubra in July when the Dalai Lama goes there to dedicate a new shrine. Ama le invites you to accompany her and her friends.

'I should love to,' I reply from my boulder, 'but I shall be back home by then.'

'Leave after the apricot harvest. In August, these will start to drop from their branches so ripe and plump (you can catch them, midair, with a teacup) that you can't see the grass for all that red. Then in September, the apples …'

Her voice recedes. In the vision that has conjured itself, Ama le is seated right where she is, apricots swirling in slow motion around her like satellites. Butterflies too, trailing dry-brush gold mantras from their wings. The frame tilts slightly. She is a child in pigtails, a sprite through the trees, transforming to a silver-gelatin studio-portrait and then fast-forward to her wedding-day in an heirloom perak. Babies. Grandbabies. Something about crowds these days. I reluctantly return to the moment.

'Crowds where, Ama le?'

'At Hemis gompa, beta. Too many people. Ama le is tired this year for the festival there.'

The two-day-long festival is a few days away. I've been contemplating the touristy-thing for a change of scene and pace.

'If I go,' I say, 'would Ama le like to accompany me?'

She considers the idea for a moment. 'Ama le has attended the festival a number of times; it would be nice to witness again, especially the masked dances. Do you know them?'

'I have a vague idea,' I reply.

'Ah they are unique, the monks all dressed up as creatures from bad dreams with fierce faces. As they dance in the courtyard, we memorize the faces so that they cannot frighten us when we meet them in the afterlife. It is always the same dances, the same parables. Because some of us will pass away before the festival next year, it is good to reacquaint ourselves with the creatures while we can. Ama le will let you know if she feels up to it; you must go even if she cannot.'

A change of topic is in order; something less batty.

'By the way, Ama le, when I was up at Market Road a while back, a whole lot of people had assembled along the pavements leading to Chokhang Vihara. Pin drop silence, everyone waiting, the women with strange fabulous silk flowers in their tall hats and more of the same in their hands. I was beginning to wonder whether anything would at all happen when a band appeared round the corner playing drums and trumpets followed by an air force jeep and some more vehicles. Riding in the front with the driver was a sweet old Rinpoche wearing sunglasses exactly like mine.'

'A Rinpoche? Today? Are you sure?'

'Absolutely. The procession stopped outside the vihara. The Rinpoche climbed out of the jeep; the chief constable and some lamas stepped forward for his blessings and then ushered him in followed by the rest. Mr Wangnoo and I stood watching from his steps with our cups of tea.'

'When did all this happen?'

'Maybe an hour and a half back.'

'The prayers would have commenced,' she frets, trying to get off the boulder. 'How could Ama le have forgotten. Quick! Help Ama le up.'

A lemon-coriander chicken for lunch salvages loss-of-face incurred over irrigation channels. Following a catnap, Yangchan and Wangial have returned to the fields. When they are done there, the water will be led onwards in the evening to the neighbours. They must repeat the drill next week when it is released to Upper Tukcha Road again.

Tsering Wangmo is still at school. Ama le, we know, will be back late from the temple. I make myself a cup of tea and get on with puréeing some tomatoes and garlic with Kashmiri chilli powder (for enhanced colour, not heat) to marinate the other chicken for a dinnertime experiment. I then chop some onions and mince some ginger, do the dishes, dry out the casserole, wipe down the cooking range, rinse out the dishcloth, align the spice jars, tidy the counters, put away the knives and settle down in the glass-room with another cup of Assam.

A drowsy hush has settled over the house – a particular quiet that visits around this time and alters the light and silences the magpies. Mme David-Néel is lying face down on a divan where she'd been deserted post breakfast. I repair with her to a dhukhang in Tibet.

> Hanging from the high ceiling, from the galleries and against the tall pillars, scrolls of painting show countless Buddhas and deities, while a host of other worthies, saints, gods, and demons may be vaguely discerned on the frescoes which decorate the walls of the dark edifice.
>
> At the bottom of the hall, behind rows of butter lamps, shine softly the gilded images of former Grand Lamas and the massive silver and gold reliquaries which contain their ashes or mummified bodies.

The only dhukhangs I've visited were in Lamayuru and Alchi. Surely, that life-like figure in the cave at the former was a mummy? And then that frightful monkey paw, our first evening in Leh. I still can't believe a full year has whizzed by.

The peaks of Stok are shadowing over early today. Thoughts wander to Ama le and our conversation under the apricot trees. It's probably too late for Chokhang Vihara. I should have followed Rinpoche & Co in, witnessed a ceremony, perhaps, but doing so would have invariably delayed kitchen duties. Oh well. I turn back to the page, but my mind is a monkey and refuses to concentrate. I set the book aside. The sound of running feet, and the door of the glass-room flies open with a bang. It is Tsering, breathless and anxious, with Tommy close behind.

'Pleasequickly,' she gasps, flinging down her satchel and school cap and dashing into the kitchen. 'Imustmakeanomelette.'

'An omelette?' I frown. 'There's some chicken left –'

'No! Not for me! For them!' she wails, launching into a Hindi lament, the gist of which, under the circumstances, is a bit preposterous: my *poor* father and mother are *so* hungry and tired working *so* hard *all* day in the *hot* sun I *must* take them an aloo omelette before they starve to *death* the *bechaarey* etcetera etcetera.

Pay no attention, I tell myself, and the histrionics will subside. But no. She's kicking up an infernal racket in there, with Tommy pitching in with sharp hysterical yaps. It would be so satisfying to pick them both up and drop them out of the window. I levitate from the divan and across the glass-room.

The kitchen looks like it's been hit by a typhoon, scattering eggs and assorted vegetables from their baskets. An empty saucepan is starting to smoke on a high flame. The dog is chasing an egg. The child is clutching a knife.

'Save the theatrics, Miss Gangba,' I say carefully, turning off the gas. This has all the potential to get out of hand. The neurotic dog, first. I tell him to sit and he promptly sprawls frog-flat, smiling up and wagging. 'Good boy. Now you – '

The small human being is studying me with an odd expression for a ten-year-old face. When it speaks, it is to tell me in a cold level voice how hard we must all work and to not get *gussa* with a little child.

The nerve. 'Good,' I smile, kindly. 'Out, now, both of you. Scram.'

'But I have to –' she begins, and then: Come, Tommy le. Let us not trouble poor Vikram le while he makes a *big* omelette.

I can do with a stiff drink this evening. A cigarette too would be excellent. In the absence of either, I am nursing a thimble of light Assam. Our guests have arrived.

Jigmet, back from a field-visit to Ulley in the Sham Valley, looks younger and more elfin each time he pops by. Perhaps he owns a private fountain of youth. Or perhaps it has everything to do with scampering about the great outdoors after snow leopards and the like. He is accompanied today by his children: a serious young man of nineteen and two younger ladies. The son could pass for a kid brother of his parent. The daughters have inherited their dad's mischievous twinkle. The older of the two has brought along a book. The youngest and the child of the house are snickering in a corner over the latter's *Tintin in Tibet*.

'Jigmet, I am still waiting to try some chang.'

'Ah yes; we must get you some.'

'You said exactly the same thing last week. I leave on the thirtieth.'

'The next time you are here, then, definitely.'

'I've heard that before as well. Is it so difficult to organise? Or are you worried I'll get completely plastered?'

'We aren't too concerned about that,' he laughs. 'It's just that it is hard to find a fresh batch. You'll be back anyway to do the walks next season. You can celebrate with plenty of chang when you finish.'

We live in hope. The reference is to two treks, one in the Sham and the other through Hemis National Park, that Man and I had plans for this summer. From meticulous descriptions of these on the SLC website, the set trails, graded 'easy to moderate' and 'moderate to strenuous', demand a fair level of fitness (and survival skills, common sense, sense of humour, self-assurance) to take on six to eight days of vast open wilderness, with nights spent in tiny villages along the trails. In a fuzzy little vignette that has materialized over my head, Man and I are chang-ing past flying lamas and yetis, keeping left of chortens, Tommy resolutely leading the way.

'Evil thoughts as usual?' says Yangchan, emerging from the kitchen with a mountain of basmati to accompany the chicken curry. Wangial's contribution is his trademark lemony tomato-onion-cucumber-carrot-coriander salad.

Ama le's dinner is taken to her room so I don't get a chance to ask after her day. It is late by the time Jigmet and his brood leave. Miss Gangba has fallen asleep on a divan.

'Julley for taking over the kitchen today,' says Wangial, carrying the sleeping monster to bed. 'The omelette too was very welcome. She said you insisted on making it.'

There is no mistaking the figure selecting postcards in Leh-Ling Bookshop. It feels like it was only yesterday that we met at the telephone booth.

'Is your novel published?' says the Rev Oxblood.

'I'm flattered that you remember.'

'The moment you stepped in.' He makes a fan of his selection. 'For my nieces and nephews. What do you think?'

The postcards are of Deskit-dune Bactrians, chapped-cheeked Ladakhi brats, apple blossoms, a party of woolly-masked dancers who look more comic than fierce.

'Very sweet. I'm thinking of going there.'

'To Amsterdam?'

'To Hemis. The family I'm staying with, the grandmother, actually, says it's good karma to see these chaps in the flesh before we meet them in the afterlife.'

'Go prepared for plenty of shoving and pushing, perhaps even a stampede. I mean in Hemis.'

'She mentioned crowds as well. In Hemis,' I laugh, nervously.

'A nightmare nowadays. This isn't the year for the large thangka. Still, you'll see the smaller one unrolled down the front of the gompa. But you probably know this already?'

'Guru Padmasambhava.' A giant thangka embroidered, not painted, with a jewel-studded representation of the eighth-century Buddhist teacher is displayed at the seventeenth-century gompa once every twelve years. The next showing is scheduled for 2016.

'That is correct. Now, coming back to your novel. Would I find it on these shelves?'

'Not a chance,' I begin. 'Let's just say everything changed the morning after we met.' That he's been in my thoughts every day since is a detail I feel no need to furnish. Yet. 'If we could exchange addresses, there is something I must send you. When it's done, of course, whenever that may be.'

The monk smiles. 'Certainly. I always enjoy a good surprise.'

Khambir, like all breads, is sacred, and like all breads, the mainstay of the local cuisine. Preparing the dough for the following day's batch is the last ritual of each evening.

In a large mixing bowl, Yangchan combines three teacups of unbleached wheat flour, half a teaspoon of dry yeast, a big pinch of salt and a cup of warm water into a basic dough that requires no kneading. It is left in the bowl, covered with cling film, to prove overnight.

Breakfast time. Knock back the dough. Divide it into eight pieces and shape them into balls, a little larger than ping-pong ones, ensuring there are no cracks. Allow these to rest on a lightly floured board for a couple of minutes. Meanwhile, place a non-stick skillet on a low flame.

Flatten each ball – not by rolling but by clapping between the palms – to a ¼-inch disc. Lay it on the skillet, allowing thirty seconds on either side. Pop the disc directly onto the burner for a couple of seconds and, with a pair of tongs, move it evenly over the flame. When the disc puffs up from the heat, turn it over so that the other side may receive its kiss of the flame.

Khambir, like all breads, must be broken and shared. Heavenly, warm, with butter and honey. When cold, the ideal pocket for a crunchy salad.

Although I'd set my heart on it the very first morning, I've been putting off the actual purchase. It's done now. Sloe Eyes makes a neat parcel of the kilim, folding it to the heft of a large dictionary that I can comfortably carry as cabin baggage. As I leave, Mr Wangnoo hands me three one-gram boxes of Kashmir saffron.

'The very best quality,' he says.

'Until next year,' I say, shaking hands.

Back at the homestead, they are itching to see the latest indulgence. We inaugurate it in my room with tea and cookies. The afternoon barges in to reveal more reds in the weave than I had originally counted. What is it about this colour, trailing me everywhere?

The forty-something kilometre drive from Leh has taken just over an hour, part of it on a stretch of highway that Man and I had taken to Pang Gong and Tso Moriri. Ama le's stayed behind – another dizzy spell yesterday – so it's just Namgyal the cabbie and I, not a shred of conversation between us as we course past the mani at the crossroads with the sentry, past Choglamsar's bustle of Tibetan shops and restaurants, the chortens and willows along the approach to Shey, the sacred fish pond and the hydel-project, before a turn-off to the right. Onwards, then, between military installations and into a series of low ranges.

The mouth of a narrow valley, invisible from the distance, is guarded by crumbled chortens. The valley itself is a surprise of trees, bridges and dwellings, typically higgledy-piggledy, all of it dominated by a low-slung edifice in the jagged hillside. It is a little past 8 a.m. when we pull up outside the gompa of Hemis.

With less than twenty-four hours to go before the festival commences, there are few obvious signs that the place will be teeming with people over the following two days. I wonder, just for a moment, if I've been too hasty in deciding to forego the event based on second-hand and, for all I know, overblown opinions regarding crowds and stampedes.

A flight of steps from the parking lot has brought us to the main gateway into the complex. It opens onto an enormous courtyard, enclosed on three sides by colonnaded galleries on two levels and, to the right, the palatial three-storeyed principal façade of the monastery. A grand stairway there is flanked by two long cloisters of prayer wheels; there's another stairway further ahead. The entire structure, including the cloisters and the galleries, is trimmed with silken bunting. In a corner of the courtyard is a stack of barricades, waiting to be arranged. Already in place in the galleries are hundreds of plastic chairs; the loggias above must be similarly filled. A central pavilion, rising through both levels of galleries and facing the monastery, houses an elaborately decorated plinth.

'For Rinpoche's throne, tomorrow,' says Namgyal, following my gaze.

Set in a line in the middle of the courtyard are three exceptionally tall wooden posts bearing tarchens, their shadows scoring diagonals across the paving. Barring two monks who emerge from somewhere and move out of sight, the whole place appears to be deserted. Namgyal indicates a staircase to a side. 'Guru lhakhang, first,' he says.

I follow him up, pausing for a second at the landing. The first-floor galleries are indeed full of chairs, packed to the very edges of the balconies. The next flight climbs up a dim stairwell with knee-high risers and narrow treads. To be caught here in a squash would be a nightmare. But then, had I come here tomorrow with festivities in full swing, it's unlikely I'd have made it anywhere beyond the courtyard.

The terrace we've arrived on is hemmed by apartments – a sort of elevated inner courtyard, at an intermediate level in the pile. I am struck, not for the first time, by how much these gargantuan buildings resemble rolltop desks in their architecture of pigeonholes and tiers, hidden compartments and long-forgotten crevices, so many intrigues behind their implacable façades. I wonder which would be more frightening: to be lost in a gompa or misplaced in a desk. Namgyal has left his shoes at a door in the terrace. I slip out of my sandals and duck in after him.

The dimensions are unexpected. The double-height chamber, maybe eighty feet from floor to ceiling, is dominated at the far end by an immense seated image, rendered with a fierce stare and vivid polychromes. Guru Padmasambhava, tutelary guardian of the monastery, is framed by towering wooden columns and brocaded banners. It takes a moment to distinguish between fabric that is real and that which is painted plasterwork; the figure's garments are styled as a chinoiserie of vajras and frills. One of Padmasambhava's slippered feet rests on a lotus pad, held up, at ground level, by a glowering, human-scale figure. A number of katas are draped over the arms of this personage. More scarves are piled on the lotus-throne plinth of the main image. I watch with interest as Namgyal takes out two new katas from his shoulder bag and adds them to the offerings. He then prostrates thrice before each image and starts to walk backwards, bowing every few steps, all the way to the door and out. I follow his example but without the prostrations and bowing – to do so would be contrived – lest it offends Namgyal or, worse, the dedicatee of the temple.

Outside, a different doorway opens onto another stretch of the terrace with a range of sooty glass windows to one side. The sound of a drum issues from a door festooned with prayer flags. Namgyal once again removes his shoes and invites me to follow.

The air in the small chamber is rancid. Seated crosslegged in the glow of some butter lamps is an ancient monk, chanting from a manuscript to the accompaniment of the drum in his hand. The instrument resembles an oversized tambourine with skins on both sides and a vertical wooden stem. The drumstick is shaped like a question mark and has the texture of a desiccated snake. The monk looks like he has been at it for centuries without a pause. A screen next to him is layered in prayer flags. A doorway in it is a dark void.

'What's in there?' I whisper to Namgyal.

'Mahakala temple,' he whispers back with a scared look in his eyes. 'We must not go in.'

The monk looks up from the manuscript and holds my gaze, all the while chanting and drumming. It all feels rather strange. After several minutes of this, Namgyal places some money in a tray of offerings and ushers me out.

The next flight of steps brings us to the roof of the gompa. The parapets are embellished with miles of prayer flags and a set of manis pretending to be weathervanes. I peer over the edge.

The courtyard below is very far away. The true height of the tarchens only now becomes evident. To keep them from keeling over, each post is tethered to the roof ridge with lengths of metal chains. My head suddenly feels heavy. I pull myself back and away from the parapet. At the same time, a weird rustling rises from the lower levels of the gompa, as though an army of beetles has been unleashed through it. The sound grows – voices, running feet, something metallic – and abruptly fades to complete silence.

'Sir, quick,' calls Namgyal from behind me.

Before I can reply, he has scampered down the steps. There is nothing for it but to race after him. A shortcut down the warren brings us, past the empty courtyard, to the grand stairway in the façade. The pavilion at the top is strewn with footwear in a bewildering array of types and sizes to which we add our pairs. Two enormous red doors with ornate brass studs have been pushed wide open. A red velvet curtain is gathered in silk cord down the middle of the doorway. I step over the threshold. My timing is perfect.

Epilogue

The pads of the drumsticks are a hair's breath away from the drumskins. It is the same with the cymbals, poised in the monks' hands. The long horns are supported under their chins on carved wooden collars.

At a sign from a monk in the middle of the gathering, the drums establish a murmured rhythm, picked up by a shiver of cymbals and deep long moans from the long *dung-chens*. The *gyalings*, trumpeting their presence by the throne platform, are reminiscent of geese long ago. To a whirl of bells, the chanting begins. The wind instruments become a multiphonic accompaniment, expressing three notes of a chord that underscores the measured formality of the proceedings. I've sunk to the floor to sit crosslegged in an aisle; the huddled figures fore and aft jostle and fidget even as they sing from the manuscripts open before them.

The child-monks must rise through the ranks to someday occupy the front benches. Any one of them may embody the qualities of a future Rinpoche, in which case his place is already assured on the elevated spot to the left of this vantage point. For now, the children are restricted to the last two rows along the perimeter of the dhukhang. In the murals behind them are hundreds of Buddhas, their radiance scarcely muted by the soot of three centuries.

A different aisle separates the child-monks from their adolescent peers and another aisle, ahead, the boys from the men. The latter are themselves segregated by age and precedence, to either side of the broadest aisle, directly under the Rinpoche's gaze.

The square atrium in the middle of the dhukhang is cascaded with thangkas of exquisite antiquity and artistry, yards of brocade and a shaft of daylight. The sun has devised a way of reaching between the suspended textiles and the great wooden columns to cast its eyes around every corner of the assembly. The other sources of light are groupings of butter lamps, flickering at dodo-level along the murals enclosing the assembly. More butter lamps are ranged at the altar facing the main door from the opposite side, and around a chorten-shrine to the right of the atrium. The altar is seated with a large, gilded and partially veiled divinity. The chorten-shrine is surrounded by diminishing tiers of tsogs.

In an interlude to the proceedings, the air fills with the susurration of the child-monks and a ragtag group of lay people who come to occupy the same aisle. The biddies that constitute the bulk of the party have probably timed their entry with the monks' tea break; the women have brought their own plastic mugs, held at the ready in wizened hands. The child-monks too have produced mugs from the folds of their garments. Already, a clutch of novices is making their way between the front ranks, bearing great silver jugs with gold dragons for handles and spouts like beaks. By the time they reach the aisle with the biddies, the drone of chants has once again commenced. Its spell is sustained for close to sixty minutes.

In the lead to the last cycle of prayers, the novices once again move between the aisles, this time with trays of lit butter lamps. When every member of the clergy, the children included, has a butter-lamp in his hand, the dung-chens mark the start of a grand psalmody. The canticles rise and swell and all but lift the thangkas and brocades suspended from the central well of light. The light itself is now plumed with smoke from bundles of incense passed from hand to hand. The sounds surge and echo from the painted walls and the ceiling, building to a coda of bells, big drums and little drums, gyalings and dung-chens.

It ends so abruptly that my ears are deafened by the silence.

The butter lamps have been set down. Each monk reaches for a folded object that has, until this moment, remained untouched on the low tables before them, all along sharing space with the manuscripts, cups, cymbals and bells. In one slow synchronized move, the folds open to become wide conical hats like a field of poppies in timeless time lapse.

One by one, row by row, the monks rise to their feet, step forward to receive the blessings of their Rinpoche. It's the turn, last, of the laity. Unbeknown to me, Namgyal has brought two katas for us to present. Rinpoche has a smile of infinite kindness.

Shortly, outside.

The flagstones are burnt by the sun to the colour of bone ash. In the time we've spent inside the dhukhang, the shadows of the tarchens in the middle of the courtyard have shrunk to mere blips on the ground. Seven monks have disposed themselves in an arc around the central flagpole. One of the great tambourines on stalks has been called into service. To a steady beat from the drum – how different it sounds out here in the open – the monks practice their dances for the festival that will celebrate the Solstice. That they dance today in their everyday robes, minus masks and trappings of any sort, lends the spectacle an unexpected dimension.

Three slow loping strides in a clockwise curve. A slow, slow, clockwise turn on the right foot. The arms are held high with elbows angled. The wrists inscribe a fluid twirl. Three strides forward and another spot turn. The figures may be manis, spinning on their axes. Or strange dark birds, chasing their shadows. The arc completes its cycle around the tarchen, and starts to inscribe another circumference. It goes on and on, without a pause.

In time, the monk in the lead enters a world of his own – several light steps ahead of the others. There is a point where his form casts no shadow on the ground. That's when he appears to be a levitating monk.

Julley!

To ten States of India, up and down
The Golden Quadrilateral and BRO

Jigmet Dadul and Radhika Kothari at Snow Leopard Conservancy
Sonam Gyaphel, the Gangbas and the Rev Oxblood

For chocolate, tipple, White Clouds, Redbox,
InDesign, addresses and fingers crossed:

Arathi Abraham, Devika and Chitrajit Cariapa, Brinda Datta,
Priya Ganapathy and Anurag Mallick, Rajashi Ghosh, Surabhi Gurukar,
Nirada Harendra, Sandhya Harendra, Pheroza Hataria, Chaitanya Hegde,
Sachindra Karanth, Meher Kharas, Abha Kohli and Francis Joseph, Ryan Lobo,
Pradeep Narrain, Gitto Patni, Nirmala Rudra, Mira Seth, Sudeshna Shome-Ghosh,
Simhendra and Amartya and Sreya and Yogendra Urs

To Kuruvilla Abraham
friend, literary agent, diamond

To Karthika V.K. at HarperCollins India
and to my editors Ajitha G.S. and Amit Dixit

To one aunt, two sets of mums and dads, a spouse and two brothers
And two more Inimitables: P.Singh and Manoj Bawa

Glossary

abi: grandmother

ama: mother

amchi: (m/f) traditional doctor

bok: scarf

chang: barley beer

chen: big

chipa: bird

chogtse: low, carved wooden table

chorten: the characteristic Tibetan Buddhist votive or reliquary stupa

chu: water; also river

chung: small

chu-tagie: lit. water-bread; a vegetable and/or mutton stew with wholewheat dumplings

dhukhang: the assembly hall of a gompa

don: have, partake of

drimo: cow yak

dzo/dzomo (m/f): draught-animal, crossed from a yak and a cow

gompa: Tibetan Buddhist monastery

goncha: gown

gyaling: ritual trumpet

gyogspa: hurry up!

kahwa: traditional Kashmiri tea

kata: ceremonial Tibetan scarf

katangputit: magpie

khambir: pita-like wholewheat bread

khang: house

kilim: flat-weave rug

le: respectful suffix to names, actions

lha tho: votive cairn

lhakhang: the prayer hall of a monastery; temple

mani: prayer wheel; also, stone carved with sacred inscriptions

meme: grandfather

mok mok: steamed or deep-fried dumpling with vegetable or meat filling

ol: lucerne; alfalfa

perak: headgear decorated with semi-precious stones

phia: marmot

Rinpoche: lit. Precious One; high lama

rulag: sheep, goats

shan: snow leopard

solja: butter tea

tarchen: vertical prayer flag

tarchok: the five-colour prayer flags, strung horizontally or at a slight diagonal

tenmo: bear

thangka: votive scroll, painted with Buddhist divinities

thul: egg

trapa: married monk

tsampa: barley flour

tsepo: backpack-basket

tsogs: ceremonial offering of tsampa combined with butter and dry fruit

Twenty-One Taras: Aspects of the female Buddha or Bodhisattva, invoked by a specific mantra to the (1) Chief Green Tara; (2) Tara who Saves from All Calamities; (3) Tara who Saves from Earthquakes; (4) Tara who Saves from Water Calamities; (5) Tara who Saves from Fire Calamities; (6) Tara who Saves from Wind Calamities; (7) Tara who Increases Property and Wisdom; (8) Tara who Saves from Sky Calamities; (9) Tara who Saves from War; (10) Tara who Saves from Prison; (11) Tara who Saves from Robbers; (12) Tara who Increases Power; (13) Tara who Saves from Demons; (14) Tara who Saves from Calamities to Livestock; (15) Tara who Saves from Wild Beasts; (16) Tara who Saves from Poison; (17) Tara who Subdues Great Demons; (18) Tara of Medicine; (19) Tara of Longevity; (20) Tara of Wealth; (21) Tara who Fulfils all Wishes

vajra: thunderbolt

yul: village

yulpa: villager

zhankey: long-haired mountain dog

Bibliography

Allen, Charles, *The Buddha and the Sahibs*, John Murray, London, 2003

David-Néel, Alexandra, *Magic & Mystery in Tibet*, Rupa, New Delhi, 2007

Goepper, Roger, *Alchi*, Shambhala, Boston, 1996

Govinda, Lama Anagarika, *The Way of the White Clouds*, Overlook, New York, 2005

Gurung, K.K., and Raj Singh, *Mammals of the Indian Subcontinent and Where to Watch Them*, Indian Experience, Oxford, 1996

Hart-Davis, Duff, *Honorary Tiger: The Life of Billy Arjan Singh*, Lotus-Roli, New Delhi, 2005

Hergé, *Tintin in Tibet*, Methuen, London, 1977

Kazmierczak, Krys, *A Field Guide to the Birds of India*, Om Books, New Delhi, 2006

Michell, George, *Penguin Guide to the Monuments of India, Vol. 1: Buddhist, Jain, Hindu*, Penguin, London, 1991

Norman, Rebecca, *Getting Started in Ladakhi: A Phrasebook for Learning Ladakhi*, Melong Publications, Leh, 2001

Pfister, Otto, *Birds and Mammals of Ladakh*, Oxford University Press, New Delhi, 2004

Rizvi, Janet, *Ladakh: Crossroads of High Asia*, Oxford University Press, New Delhi, 1996

Tzareva, Elena, *Rugs and Carpets of Central Asia*, Allen Lane/Penguin Books, Middlesex, 1984

Copyright Acknowledgements

The publisher would like to thank the following for permission to reproduce copyright material:

Page 161: Janet Rizvi, *Ladakh: Crossroads of High Asia*, Oxford University Press India, New Delhi, 1996

Pages 196 and 213: Alexandra David-Neél, *Magic & Mystery in Tibet*, Rupa & Co., New Delhi, 2008